Intelligent Business

Skills Book

Elementary
Business English

| Christine Johnson |

Pearson Education Limited
Edinburgh Gate
Harlow
Essex CM20 2JE
England
and Associated Companies throughout the world.

www.pearsonelt.com

First published 2008
Sixth impression 2015

Intelligent Business Elementary Skills Book and CD-ROM pack.
ISBN-13: 978-1-4058-8141-8

Set in Economist Roman 10.5 / 12.5

Printed by CPI UK

Acknowledgements
The publishers would like to thank the following people for their helpful comments on the manuscript for this book: Louise Bulloch, Intercom Language Services GmbH, Hamburg; Steve Bush, The British Institute, Florence; Shauna Hunter, Transfer Formation Conseil, Paris; Curtis Mackenzie, Vision Consulting Services KK, Tokyo; Nigel McGloin, Kennedy Executive Language Solutions, Madrid.

The publishers would like to thank the following people for their help in piloting and developing this course: Richard Booker and Karen Ngeow, University of Hong Kong; Adolfo Escuder, EU Estudios Empresariales, University of Zaragoza; Wendy Farrar, Università Cattolica del Sacro Cuore, Piacenza; Andrew Hopgood, Linguarama, Hamburg; Ann-Marie Hadzima, Dept of Foreign Languages, National Taiwan University, Taiwan; Samuel C. M. Hsieh, English Department, Chinese Culture University, Taipei; Laura Lewis, ABS International, Buenos Aires; Maite Padrós, Universitat de Barcelona; Giuliete Aymard Ramos Siqueira, São Paulo; Richmond Stroupe, World Language Center, Soka University, Tokyo; Michael Thompson, Centro Linguistico Università Commerciale L. Bocconi, Milan; Krisztina Tüll, Európai Nyelvek Stúdiója, Budapest.

Photo Acknowledgements
The publishers are grateful to the following for their permission to reproduce copyright photographs.

(Key: b-bottom; c-centre; l-left; r-right; t-top)

A1 PIX: 6, 7, 35; Alamy Images: Frances M. Roberts 42t, 45; imagebroker 38; Art Directors and TRIP photo Library: Helene Rogers 42 (1); Juliet Highet 51; Mountain Sport Photography 64; AXA: 15t; Bike-in-a-bag: 44 (4); Corbis: Bruce Benedict/Transtock 42 (2); Deepak Buddhiraja/India Picture 3tl, 10, 34; Fridmar Damm/zefa 54l; Image Source 28; ImageShop 3bl, 24; Jose Luis Pelaez, Inc 70; moodboard 48, 50; Pinto/zefa 13; Redlink 103; DK Images: 53; David Murray and Jules Selmes 27; Gabor Barka 54r; John See 43t; Getty Images: Bill Pugliano/Stringer 42 (3); DAJ 66, 68; Stone/Jen Petreshock 5, 62, 65; Taxi/Chabruken 56, 59; Hyundai: 15b; iStockphoto: 8c, 8l, 8r, 32b; KMX Karts Ltd: 43b; Pearson Education: 20, 44 (1), 44 (2); PunchStock: Bananastock 3br, 52; Digital Vision 14, 17, 32t; www.cleverlittleideas.com: 44 (3)

Cover images: Front: Corbis: ImageShop l; Pinto/zefa c; Getty Images: Stone/Jen Petreshock r

All other images © Pearson Education

Picture Research by: Louise Edgeworth

Illustrated by Simon Rogers, John Stainton, Tony Wilkins

Designed by David Bainbridge

Contents

Unit 2

Talk about jobs

This unit helps you to introduce other people at work. You can also learn how to describe your job. **Page 10.**

Unit 5

Go to a restaurant

This unit helps you to understand a simple menu and order a meal. You can also learn how to offer food and drink to your guests. **Page 24.**

On the inside back cover of this book you will find an interactive CD-ROM with extra activities and audio files. There is also a reference section with grammar, culture notes and good business practice information.

Unit 9

Describe products

This unit helps you to describe different kinds of products, explain what they do and say why they are special. You can also practise giving your opinion about certain products. **Page 42.**

The *Intelligent Business Elementary Skills Book* will help you develop language and skills that are important in common business situations, for example: talking about your company, describing a project and making arrangements.

The book is for elementary learners who are already in work, or are preparing for a career in business.

How can the book be used?

The Skills Book can be used alone, or with the *Intelligent Business Elementary Coursebook*. Each Skills Book unit builds on the language introduced in the Coursebook and practises that language in the context of everyday business situations. Units are designed to take 90 to 120 minutes, but learners who have not studied the Coursebook may need more time to study the grammar and vocabulary. The *Intelligent Business Elementary Workbook* will be useful for this.

The Skills Book can be taught as a one-week intensive course of 30 hours. Or, it can be used for classes that attend once or twice a week over a longer period. It is designed for groups of four to eight students, but can be adapted for use with larger groups, or with one-to-one students. (See *Intelligent Business Elementary Teacher's Book* for guidelines.)

What is in the units?

Each unit contains three practical speaking tasks, which have specific objectives, for example giving opinions or explaining a problem. Each unit also has listening activities. These provide a useful model of language and help you to develop your listening skills. The key language for each unit can be found in *What do you say?* There is a section called *Building vocabulary*, which will help you to learn the words you need for the speaking tasks and will also increase your vocabulary generally. Units start with a *Warm up* (apart from Unit 1) to help you focus on the main topic, and end with a *Summary* so that you can check what you have learned.

There are five writing units in the book which introduce the kinds of writing that are important for business: emails, simple letters, simple reports, messages and notes. You can go to the *Grammar reference* for information about the key grammar points, and for exercises to help you practise these points. In *Strategies*, you can find practical tips on how to say numbers and dates (for example), as well as useful phrases for social situations, meetings, telephoning and short presentations. You can find extra practice activities on the integrated CD-ROM. You can also use the CD-ROM to practise listening to the dialogues from each unit.

I hope you enjoy using this book and that it will help you to improve your English. Good luck!

Christine Johnson

Bookmap

Unit 13
Suggest ideas
This unit gives you key language for making suggestions and discussing ideas. You can also practise holding a short meeting.
Page 62.

Unit 1 | Make the first contact

| Introduce yourself | Check information | Introduce yourself at reception |

Task 1A
Individually

Objective: Introduce yourself to a partner

Step 1 Preparation

Complete the conversation with your personal information.

A: Hello. I'm _____ [your name]. I'm from _____ [your country].
I'm with _____ [your company].

OR

I'm a student at _____ [your school, college or university].

B: Nice to meet you.

Pairs

Step 2 Practice

Introduce yourself to the person next to you. Use the phrases from the conversation above. Practise again with one or two other people sitting near you.

Building vocabulary

Jobs

1 Which of these jobs do you know? Use a dictionary to help you.

accountant   architect   engineer   finance manager
lawyer   sales manager   receptionist   secretary

2 What other jobs do you know? What is your job title in English?

Task 1B
Whole class

Objective: Introduce yourself to the class

 Introduce yourself to the rest of your class. Say your name, nationality, company and job. If you are not in work, choose a company and job that you would like to have.

2 What are the different jobs of the people in your group? What are the different nationalities?

CD 1 ⊙ Listening 1

1 Three people arrive for a company training course. Listen to them introducing themselves. Are they all different nationalities?

2 Listen again. Are these statements true or false? Correct the false statements.

1　Mr Morris is American.　　　　*False – He's British.*
2　Ms Davidsson is British.
3　The German is a sales manager.
4　The British man is a finance manager.
5　Two people are sales managers.

3 Listen again and write the first name of the British man.

Grammar reference: *to be*, page 83

What do you say? 1

Checking information

1 Match the questions 1–8 with the answers a–h.

1　Are you British?	a　Tony Wilson.
2　Where are you from?	b　W-I-L-S-O-N.
3　What company are you with?	c　Yes. I'm an engineer.
4　Sorry, what's your company name again?	d　It's BP.
5　What's your job?	e　I'm an engineer.
6　Can you say that again?	f　I'm with BP.
7　What's your name?	g　No, I'm not.
8　Sorry, can you spell that?	h　I'm from Canada.

2 Practise the questions and answers with a partner.

Strategies: Introducing yourself, page 76

Task 2
Pairs

Objective: Check information

1 **Find out about your partner. Follow the instructions below.**

- Take turns to ask and answer questions (see 1–8 on page 7) to find out the name, company, job and nationality of your partner. Write the information in the table. Ask your partner to spell his/her name and company name. Check the information: ask your partner to say difficult words again.
- Student A turn to page 97.
- Student B write the information in the table below.

2 **Change roles and repeat the task.**

- Student B turn to page 102.
- Student A write the information in the table below.

Name	
Company	
Job	
Nationality	

CD 2 ⊙ Listening 2

1 **A visitor to a company comes to the reception desk and introduces himself. Listen to the conversation and answer the questions.**

1 Does the visitor want to see Sonia Brown or Julia Brown?
2 Where is Mrs Brown at the moment?
3 Complete the receptionist's question:
  Can you wait about _____ minutes?
4 At the end of the conversation, the receptionist gives something to the visitor. Is it:
  a a business card?
  b a visitor's badge?
  c a cup of coffee?

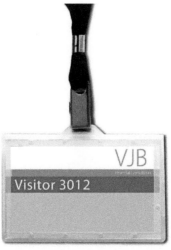

2 Listen again and complete the visitor's book with information about the visitor.

Visitors' book

Parts

Name of visitor	Company	To see	Signature
Carol Springer	Kidds & Co	Chris Maserati	C. Springer
A. Mackintosh	Red Plastics plc	Raine Lewis	A Mackintosh

What do you say? 2

At reception

Complete the conversation.

Visitor: ¹_____ morning. My ²_____ Maria Sanchez. ³_____ here to see Mr Jackson.

Receptionist: Peter Jackson or Alan Jackson?

Visitor: I'm ⁴_____ sure.

Receptionist: ⁵_____ his _____?

Visitor: Sales manager.

Receptionist: That's Peter Jackson. Just a ⁶_____. I'll call him. Hello? Reception here. Maria Sanchez is ⁷_____ to see Peter Jackson. ⁸_____ sorry, Ms Sanchez. Mr Jackson ⁹_____ in his office at the moment. ¹⁰_____ in a meeting. ¹¹_____ wait about five minutes?

Visitor: Yes, ¹²_____ _____.

Receptionist: Here is your visitor's ¹³_____. ¹⁴_____ have a seat.

Visitor: ¹⁵_____ _____.

Task 3
Pairs

Objective: Introduce yourself at reception

Role-play a conversation between a visitor and a receptionist. Take turns to be the visitor.

- Student A turn to page 97.
- Student B turn to page 100.

Summary

In this unit, you have learnt to:
- introduce yourself
- ask questions to check information
- introduce yourself at reception

Unit 2 | Talk about jobs

| Introduce someone | Introduce your team | Describe your daily routine |

Warm up

What information do you usually give about a person when you introduce them in a business situation? What information do you give in a social situation? Choose from the following.

- [ ] name
- [ ] home town
- [ ] nationality
- [ ] company
- [ ] family
- [ ] interests
- [ ] job title
- [ ] department (e.g. finance, personnel, marketing)

CD 3 ⊙ Listening 1

1 Listen to two introductions. Which one is a business situation? What information do you hear about each person?

2 Listen again. Mark the boxes above 1 (first introduction) or 2 (second introduction).

Introducing other people

CD 3 ⊙ Tick (✓) the phrases you hear in each introduction in *Listening 1*. Listen again and check.

Intro 1	Intro 2	
☐	☐	Can I introduce ...?
☐	☐	This is ...
☐	☐	He/She lives in ...
☐	☐	He/She works for ... in the ... department
☐	☐	He/She likes ...
☐	☐	He/She is interested in ...

Grammar reference: Present simple affirmative, page 84

Task 1   Objective: Introduce someone

Individually   **Step 1 Preparation**

Write six things about yourself (personal or work, or both). Give your list to a partner.

Groups of up to 6   **Step 2 Practice**

Introduce your partner to the other people in your group, using their list. It can be a business or social situation.

Building vocabulary   ## Describing jobs

What do these people do in their jobs? Choose a verb from column A and a phrase from column B below to complete the job descriptions. Use a dictionary to help you.

1   A project co-ordinator *co-ordinates projects*.
2   A conference organiser _____.
3   A marketing executive _____.
4   A sales representative _____.
5   A customer services manager _____.
6   A personnel officer _____.
7   A finance manager _____.
8   An IT service engineer _____.

A	B
~~co-ordinates~~	new employees
works	company products
deals with	the budget
organises	computer equipment
sells	conferences
maintains	the problems of customers
controls	in marketing
hires	~~projects~~

1 **A sales manager introduces her team to a visitor. Listen and match the names with the jobs.**

Name		Job	
1	Janine Parks	a	department secretary
2	Fiona Quigley	b	conference organiser
3	Ben Thomas	c	sales manager
4	Wayne Carr	d	sales representative
5	Zoe James	e	customer services manager
6	Gina Scott	f	sales representative

2 **Listen again. Are these statements true or false?**

1 Fiona Quigley is responsible for sales in the north.
2 Ben Thomas is in charge of the sales department.
3 Zoe James is in charge of customer services.
4 Wayne Carr is responsible for communication.
5 Gina Scott is responsible for organising sales conferences.

3 **What is each person in the team responsible for?**

4 **What do Ben, Wayne and Zoe do in their jobs? Choose from the following.**

answer the telephone   answer questions   arrange meetings
organise conferences   deal with problems   travel   take messages
visit customers   work in the office

Task 2
Groups of
2 or 3

Objective: Introduce your team

1 **Each person choose a job. Introduce yourself and explain 'your' job to the rest of the group.**

- Group A choose from list A below.
- Group B choose from list B.
- Then go to the back of the book to find out the job responsibilities and main activities.

A	B
Marketing manager (Turn to page 97.)	Web designer (Turn to page 100.)
Export sales assistant (Turn to page 98.)	IT project manager (Turn to page 101.)
Advertising manager (Turn to page 104.)	IT service engineer (Turn to page 102.)

Marketing manager (Turn to page 97.)   Export sales assistant (Turn to page 98.)   Advertising manager (Turn to page 104.)   Web designer (Turn to page 100.)   IT project manager (Turn to page 101.)   IT service engineer (Turn to page 102.)

Hello. I'm [name] and I'm a/an [export sales assistant]. I'm responsible for / in charge of [sales to other countries]. In my job, I [travel a lot].

Group A + B

2 **Take turns to introduce the people in your group to another group. Remember to ask for spelling or repetition if you don't understand.**

 Strategies: Introducing other people, page 76

Task 3	Objective: Describe your daily routine

Individually

Step 1 Preparation

1 Wayne Carr, the customer services manager from *Listening 2*, describes his daily routine. Number the activities in the order that he does them each day.

- [1] **I usually travel** to work by train.
- [ ] **I leave work** at 5 or 5.30pm.
- [ ] **I start work** at 8.30am.
- [ ] **In the afternoon,** we sometimes have a team meeting.
- [ ] **The first thing I do is** read my emails.
- [ ] **In the evening,** I often go out with my colleagues.
- [ ] **I usually have lunch** at 12 o'clock.

2 Write down six or eight activities from your daily routine. Use the phrases in bold above.

Pairs or small groups

Step 2 Practice

Tell your partner or partners about your daily routine.

Summary

In this unit, you have learnt to:
- introduce someone in business and social situations
- introduce other people in your team
- describe your daily work routine

Unit 3 | Talk about companies

Warm up

People often talk about their company when they meet new contacts, for example at conferences, in sales situations or when they meet someone on an aeroplane. What kind of information do people usually give? Choose from the following.

- ☐ Company name
- ☐ Kind of company (for example: retail, services or manufacturing) or industry
- ☐ Location of headquarters
- ☐ Number of employees
- ☐ Name of the CEO
- ☐ Other? _____

Building vocabulary

Industries

Match the companies 1–8 with the industries a–h. Use a dictionary to help you. What other industries do you know?

1	Samsung	a	airline
2	Lloyds	b	retail
3	Nestlé	c	computer services
4	Qantas	d	electronics
5	Exxon Mobil	e	food production
6	Nissan	f	insurance
7	Microsoft	g	oil / petroleum
8	Wal-mart	h	car manufacturing

1 Listen to four people describing their company. Which industry does each person work in?

1 _____   2 _____

3 _____   4 _____

2 Listen again. Complete the information each person gives about their company.

1   Posies sells _____ .

2   Hassel is based in _____ .

3   The Rexoil headquarters are in _____ .

4   Kim Sung has _____ in many countries.

What do you say? 1
Pairs

Describing a company

Find information about a company at the back of the book. Use the language below to write six sentences about it. (Don't tell your partner about your company yet.)

Student A: Axa (Turn to page 99.)

Student B: Hyundai (Turn to page 100.)

The company is called ...

It's a manufacturing / retail / services company.

It produces ... / sells ... / develops ... / makes ...

It's an American / a Japanese / a French / [other nationality] *company.*

It's based in [country].

The headquarters are in [place].

Task 1
Pairs

Objective: Describe a company

1 Take turns to describe 'your' company (Axa or Hyundai) to your partner.

2 Tell your partner about the company where you work, or about another company that you know.

1 Pascual Santander talks to Helen Scott about his company, Delicias, which is based in Chile. Listen and write down the number he gives for the following.

1   Number of subsidiaries: _____

2   Number of factories: _____

3   Number of employees: _____

4   Sales: _____ USD

2 **Listen again. Number the check questions in the order that you hear them.**

☐ Can you repeat that number, please?
☐ Sorry, is that 13 or 30?
☐ Sorry, can you say that again?
☐ So, that's twelve factories?

 Strategies: Talking about numbers, page 77

Task 2
Pairs

Objective: Check numbers

Your partner will give you some numerical information about a company. Use the questions from *Listening 2* to check each number. When you are sure about the number, write it down.

– Student A use the company information below.
– Student B turn to page 100.

Koa Papers (manufactures paper products)

Subsidiaries: **40**
Factories: **9**
Employees: **11,000**
Sales: **900 million USD**

| What do you say? 2 | **Asking questions about a company** |

Match the questions with the answers.

1	What's the name of your company?	a	In the UK.
2	What kind of company is it?	b	Harry Flanagan.
3	What does it make / sell / produce?	c	No, it doesn't.
4	Where are the headquarters?	d	It's a manufacturing company.
5	Does it have subsidiaries?	e	It's called Keele Machines Ltd.
6	How many employees are there?	f	About 980.
7	What are your sales figures?	g	It makes office equipment.
8	Who is the CEO?	h	£120 million a year

 Grammar reference: Present simple negative, question and short answer, page 84

Task 3

Objective: Exchange company information

Talk about company information. Follow the instructions below.

- Take turns to ask and answer questions about a company. If you don't have the answer, you can say *I don't know*. Ask your partner questions and write the information in the profile below. Remember to check numbers and spelling.
- Student A turn to page 97.
- Student B turn to page 101.

Company profile

Company name	
Kind of company or industry	
Products / Services	
Location of headquarters	
Subsidiaries	
Number of offices / stores	
Location of offices / stores	
Number of employees	
Sales	
Name of CEO	

Summary

In this unit, you have learnt to:
- describe your company
- give numbers and check numbers
- ask and answer questions about other companies

Writing 1 | Emails 1

| Introduce yourself | Write an email with questions |

What do you write? 1

1 Read the following information.

When you join a new team, it is usual to introduce yourself.
Some teams don't meet very often because they work in different places.
These team members usually communicate by phone and email.

2 Sanjay Bidi joins a team of computer consultants and introduces himself. Read the email and complete the table below with information about Sanjay.

Delete   Junk   Reply Reply All Forward   Print

From: Sanjay Bidi
To: Computer consultancy team
Subject: New team member

Dear Colleagues

My name is Sanjay Bidi. I'm a new member of the computer consultancy team and I'm responsible for networks. My job is to design and build computer networks.

Let me tell you something about myself. I'm 28 years old and I'm from Agra in India. I'm a network engineer with five years' work experience. I'm interested in all kinds of new technology, and in my free time I like computer games and cricket.

Hope to meet some of you soon!

Best regards

Sanjay

Name	
Age	
Nationality	
Job title	
Job activities	
Work experience (number of years)	
Home town	
Interests	

3 Answer the questions about Sanjay's email.

1 How does Sanjay start the email?

2 How does he end it?

4 Look at some other ways to start and end emails. Mark each one S for starting and E for ending an email.

☐ *Yours sincerely* (formal)   ☐ *Dear + name*(s) (for 1 or 2 people)

☐ *Kind regards*   ☐ *Dear all* (for more than 2 people)

☐ *Hi / Hello* (informal)   ☐ *Best wishes*

Objective: Introduce yourself

You join a marketing team as a web designer. Your job is to design the company website. You have three years' experience in web design. Use other real information about yourself or make up information and write an email to introduce yourself to your new colleagues.

1 Read the following information about Jarrets.

Jarrets is a computer services company with a lot of young employees. The employees often meet in their free time and there are a number of company clubs, for example, football, table tennis, swimming, music and photography. The human resources department wants the following information about each club:

1 The club's name 4 How often members meet
2 Activities 5 Where they meet
3 Number of members 6 Name of the club's leader

2 Put these words in the correct order to make questions. Then match the questions with the points 1–6 above.

a there / are / members / How / many ?
b do / you / often / meet / How ?
c name / What / club / the / of / your / is ?
d Who / leader / the / club's / is?
e do / you / What / do ?
f meet / Where / you / do?

| Task 2

Objective: Write an email with questions

You work in the human resources department at Jarrets. Write one email that you can send to all the clubs. You can use the phrases below. Decide how to start and end the email, and add the questions.

– The human resources department wants to collect details of all the company's clubs.
– This information is useful for new employees in the company.
– Can you please answer some questions about your club?
– Many thanks for your help.

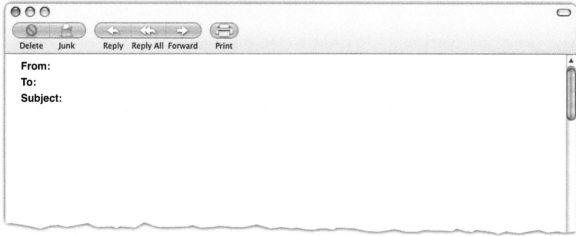

Grammar reference: Articles, page 85

Unit 4 | Give instructions and directions

| Describe location | Give instructions | Give directions |

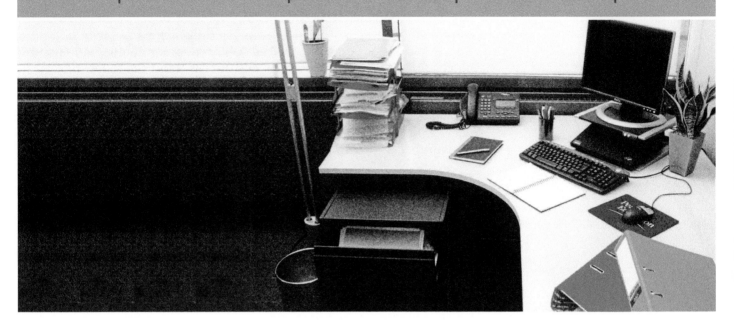

Warm up

Talk about the place where you work.

Do you work in an office, in a factory – or in another kind of place?

Do you work alone or with other people? How many people usually work in the same room?

Do you like the place where you work? Why? / Why not?

Building vocabulary

Office equipment

Match these words with the items in the picture above. Two of the things are not in the picture. Use a dictionary to help you.

desk chair PC telephone mouse files in-tray desk diary notebook filing cabinet drawer bin pen holder

---

Task 1
Pairs

Objective: Describe location

Take turns to ask and answer questions about the following.

pens	files that you don't use often
files that you use often	paperclips
mail (letters)	things you don't want

Use *keep* for the items above, for example:

Where do you keep ...?   In my desk drawer.

notes	the dates of important meetings

Use *write* for the items above, for example:

Where do you write ...?   In a notebook.

1 Are these statements about the picture opposite true or false? Correct the false statements.

1 There are no pens in the pen holder.
2 There is one file on the desk.
3 There is a pen on the notebook.
4 The notebook is in front of the phone.
5 The in-tray is next to the phone.
6 The bin is under the desk.

2 Write some more sentences to describe the picture.

 Grammar reference: Prepositions of place, page 86

Look at the picture of Michaela's office below and answer the questions.

1 Where is the cupboard?   *In the corner.*
2 Where is the filing cabinet?
3 Where is the small table?
4 How many drawers does the filing cabinet have?
5 How many shelves does the bookcase have?
6 Match the following with a, b and c in the picture.
   ☐ the middle drawer of the filing cabinet
   ☐ the bottom drawer of the filing cabinet
   ☐ the top shelf of the bookcase

CD 7 ⊙ Listening 1   **Listen to a telephone conversation between Michaela and Eva, a colleague. Michaela is in a meeting and needs an important document. She can't leave the meeting, so she asks Eva to bring it to her. Where is the document?**

Giving instructions

CD 8 **1** Listen to the first part of the conversation again. Michaela asks Eva politely to find a report and bring it to her. She doesn't say: 'Find it and bring it to me now.' What does she say?

_____ find it and bring it to me?

How does Eva answer?

1 Sorry I'm busy.   2 No problem.   3 Right.

CD 9 **2** Michaela gives several instructions to help Eva find the report. Listen to the second part of the conversation again and complete the sentences.

1 _____ into my office.
2 _____ the top drawer of the filing cabinet.
3 _____ in a file with the name 'New projects'.
4 Please _____ _____ the file.
5 Just _____ the report.

Here are some of Eva's responses to the instructions. Which one do you hear at the end of the conversation?

1 I'll do it now.   2 Right.   3 Yes.

Strategies: Instructions, page 78

Grammar reference: The imperative, page 85

Task 2
Pairs

Objective: Give instructions

1 Look at the picture of the office on page 21. You are going to give your partner instructions to find some things in the office. Follow the instructions below.

– Imagine you are talking to him/her on the telephone (sit back to back) and give instructions so he/she can find what you need.
– Student A turn to page 97 to see the things that you need and the locations.
– Student B make a note of what your partner wants and where it is.

2 Change roles and repeat the task.

– Student B turn to page 101 to see the things that you need and the locations.
– Student A make a note of what your partner wants and where it is.

Listening 2 **1** Study the map of a town centre on page 23. Tick (✓) the places you can see.

☐ car park   ☐ hotel   ☐ park   ☐ shops
☐ police station   ☐ bus station   ☐ train station

CD 10 **2** Listen to a conversation between Kathy and Alain. They are meeting for dinner at the Hong Kong restaurant. Where is the restaurant on the map? Circle the correct place a–f.

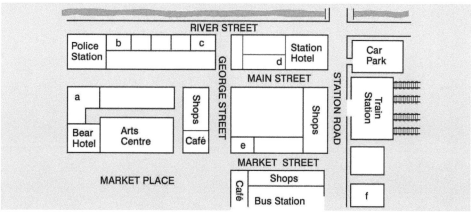

What do you say? 3

Giving directions

1 **Look at the map again and complete Kathy's directions.**

1   The restaurant is in the town centre, near *the train station*.

2   OK, so come out of the train station. Turn _____.

3   Go along _____ Road.

4   Go past the _____.

5   Take the first turning _____ and you're in River Street.

6   The _____ is on your right.

7   _____ straight on.

8   The restaurant is on the corner of _____.

Strategies: Directions, page 78

2 **Use the same map to complete the conversation.**

A: Let's meet at the Arts Centre.

B: I don't know it. Can you tell me [1]_____ it is?

A: It's in Market Place, [2]_____ _____ the Bear Hotel.

B: How do I get there from the bus station?

A: From the bus station, [3]_____ left and [4]_____ along Station Road. Take the first [5]_____ left and you are [6]_____ Market Street. Go [7]_____ Market Street and you come to Market Place. The Arts Centre is on your [8]_____.

Task 3
Pairs

Objective: Give directions

Choose a place on the map but don't say what it is. Give your partner directions to find it and tell him/her where to start from. After following the directions, your partner should say the name of the place to confirm the right answer. Then change roles and repeat the task.

Summary

In this unit, you have learnt to:

- describe where things are in your office

- give instructions politely

- ask for and give directions in a town

Unit 5 | Go to a restaurant

| Ask politely | Order food and drink | Be a polite host or guest |

Warm up

1 You are in an English-speaking restaurant. Discuss the different ways you can order coffee.

1　I want coffee.
2　I'd like a coffee, please.
3　Can I have a coffee, please?
4　Give me a coffee.

2 If you translate what you usually say in your country, is it more similar to 1, 2, 3 or 4?

　Strategies: Requests, page 79

What do you say? 1

Ordering food in a restaurant

1 Match the waiter's questions 1–4 with the responses a–d.

1　Are you ready to order?
2　What would you like to start with?
3　What would you like to drink?
4　Would you like a dessert?

a　We'd like a bottle of water, please.
b　Sorry, can we have a little more time?
c　Yes, I'd like ice cream, please.
d　Can I have soup, please?

2 Complete the requests to the waiter by matching 1–4 with a–e. 1 and 2 have two answers each.

1	I'd like / We'd like	a	the bill please.
2	Can I have	b	pay in euros?
3	Please can you bring	c	a table for four, please.
4	Can I	d	another glass?
		e	steak, please?

 Grammar reference: Modal verbs, *can* and *would*, page 87

Task 1
Pairs

Objective: Ask politely

You are in a restaurant. Take turns to ask the waiter for things, for example, a glass of water, a clean fork, the bill, a receipt, etc.

– The customer can use these phrases:

Can I have ...? / Can we have ...? / I'd like ... / We'd like ... / Can you bring ..., please?

– The waiter can reply:

Certainly. / Just a moment, please.

Building vocabulary **Food**

Create a menu using the following things. Write the names of each food or dish in the correct part of the menu. Use a dictionary to help you.

fried or roast potatoes   onion soup   chicken curry   chocolate mousse carrots   peas   fillet steak   seafood cocktail   ice cream   salad of lettuce and tomatoes   fresh fruit salad   rice   roast lamb   grilled salmon

What other dishes can you add to this menu?

Riverside
Lunch Menu

Starters

_____

_____

Main courses

_____

_____

_____

Vegetables and side dishes

_____

_____

_____

_____

Desserts

_____

_____

_____

1 **Georgio and Rossana have lunch in a restaurant in London. Listen to a conversation between Georgio, Rossana and the waiter and answer the questions.**

1   Rossana says: 'I'm sorry, but I don't like ...'. What food is she talking about?

2   What does Georgio order to drink?

2 **Listen again. What food do they order? Complete the table.**

	Georgio	Rossana
Starter		
Main course		
Vegetables or side dishes		

 Strategies: Offers and opinions, page 79

Task 2
Groups of
2 or 3

Objective: Order food and drink

1 **Use the instructions and the phrases below to role-play four short conversations.**

–   Use the menu from *Building vocabulary* to order different dishes.
–   Student A: You are the waiter / waitress in a restaurant.
–   Student B (and C): You are the customer(s).

Conversation 1

Customer:	**Waiter / Waitress:**
Ask for a table.	'Certainly. Please come this way.'
Ask for the menu/drinks list.	'Yes, of course.'

Conversation 2

Waiter / Waitress:	**Customer(s):**
'Are you ready to order?'	Say yes.
Ask what each customer would like to start with.	Order a starter.
Ask about the main course.	Order a main course.
Offer something to drink.	Order a drink.

Conversation 3

Waiter / Waitress:	**Customer:**
Ask if the customer would like a dessert.	Order a dessert.
Ask if the customer would like coffee.	Say yes or no (politely).

Conversation 4

Customer:	**Waiter / Waitress:**
Ask for the bill.	'Certainly. Here you are.'

2 **Change roles and practise again.**

Stephen Baker invites a Polish customer, Magda Gajer, to dinner at a restaurant. Listen to the conversation. Are these statements true or false? Correct the false statements.

1 Stephen often comes to this restaurant.

2 A trout is a kind of vegetable.

3 Magda doesn't like fish.

4 Magda asks for a salad.

5 Magda likes the food

What do you say? 2

Host and guest

1 **Look at the phrases a–j from *Listening 2*. In what situation can you use them? Match the situations 1–10 with the phases a–j.**

1 Host: ask what your guest would like to eat.

2 Guest: ask for a recommendation.

3 Host: give a recommendation.

4 Guest: ask for an explanation.

5 Host: give an explanation.

6 Host: say something before you start to eat.

7 Host: ask if the guest likes the food.

8 Guest: say you like the food.

9 Host: offer more food or drink.

10 Guest: accept or refuse.

a What would you like?

b I can recommend *the trout*. It's a local speciality.

c Do you like your *trout*?

d It's a kind of fish (*meat / vegetable / fruit*).

e What do you recommend?

f It's delicious … . Everything is very good.

g How about some more …?

h Enjoy your meal!

i Sorry, but I don't know '*trout*'. What is it?

j Yes, please / No, thank you.

2 **Which is a request?**

1 I like fish!

2 I'd like the fish, please.

3 **Which are offers?**

1 What would you like?

2 What do you like?

3 Do you like salad?

4 Would you like a salad?

4 **Work with a partner. Role-play some short conversations between a host and a guest using the phrases above. Work through the situations above. You can change 'trout' to another kind of dish.**

Task 3
Groups of
2 or 3

Objective: Be a polite host or guest

Role-play a business lunch. You can use the menu on page 25 or create a new one. Take turns to be the host and ask your guests what they would like to eat or drink. Guests can ask for recommendations or explanations.

Summary

In this unit, you have learnt to:

- ask politely for something in a restaurant

- order different kinds of food and drink

- be a polite host and guest

Unit 6 | Place an order

| Ask about price | Ask about stock | Place an order |

Warm up

1 What currency do you use in your country? What other currencies do you know?

2 How do you say these prices?

1 $10   2 €7.50   3 £4.95   4 $285   5 €5,650

3 Tell your partner how much you usually pay for these items in your country.

1 a litre of petrol   2 a cup of coffee   3 a copy of *The Economist*

 Strategies: Prices, page 77

What do you say? 1 **Countable or uncountable?**

1 Which of these items do we use with *a, an* or *some*?

sugar bananas litre of cooking oil chickens espresso coffee machine ice cream maker salt bottle of mineral water

2 Take turns to ask and answer questions about the price of the items in exercise 1. Use the price list to answer.

I'd like to buy a / an / some ...   *It's / They're fifty cents per / a kilo.*
How much is it? / are they?   *They're nine dollars ninety each.*
What's the price of ...?

```
PRICE LIST
-----------------------------------
Sugar              $0.50  kilo
Bananas            $2.00  kilo
Cooking oil        $2.35  litre
Chickens           $9.90  each
Espresso Coffee    $149.50
Machine
Ice Cream Maker    $56.50
Salt               $0.40 pack of 50 grams
Mineral Water      $0.57  bottle
```

 Grammar reference: Countable and uncountable nouns, page 88

<table>
<tr><td>**Task 1**
Pairs</td><td>**Objective: Ask about price**</td></tr>
</table>

Task 1
Pairs

Objective: Ask about price

1 Role-play a conversation between a buyer and a supplier. The buyer owns a new restaurant and wants to find a good supplier for the main food items he/she needs. Think of a name for the restaurant.

- Student A: You are the buyer. Introduce yourself and your restaurant and ask about the prices of the things you need. Write down the answers.
- Student B: You are the supplier. Turn to page 101 and use the prices there to answer your partner's questions.

2 Change roles and repeat the task.

- Student B: You are the buyer. Introduce yourself and your restaurant and ask abut the prices of the things you need. Write down the answers.
- Student A: You are the supplier. Turn to page 97 and use the prices there to answer your partner's questions.

Building vocabulary

Orders

1 Complete the table. Use a dictionary to help you. What other verb / noun pairs do you know?

Verb	Person	Equipment
buy	1	———————
supply	2	———————
print	printer	3
copy / photocopy	———————	4

2 Match the sentences with the pictures.

1 ☐ We have a lot of packs in stock.
2 ☐ We don't have any – we're out of stock.

a

b

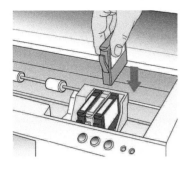

1 Silvio Santana wants to buy some cartridges for his printer. He telephones three suppliers: Stationery Plus, Quest and Plentiful Supplies. Listen and match the conversations with the situations a–c.

Call 1 ☐   Call 2 ☐   Call 3 ☐

a   The supplier has a lot of these cartridges in stock.

b   The supplier has some cartridges in stock – but not a lot.

c   The supplier is out of stock – she doesn't have any of these cartridges at the moment.

2 Listen again. Does Silvio Santana buy all twenty cartridges from one supplier? Or does he buy ten from one supplier and ten from another? Why?

What do you say? 2 *some, any, much, many*

Choose the correct word in *italics* to complete the sentences.

1   I'd like to buy *some / any* printer cartridges, please.

2   How *much / many* would you like?

3   How *much / many* are they? [to ask about price]

4   Do you have *some / any* in stock at the moment?

5   Yes, we have *some / any*.

6   I'm sorry, we don't have *some / any* at the moment – we're out of stock.

 Grammar reference: *some, any, how much/many*, page 88

Task 2	Objective: Ask about stock
Pairs	

1 You are going to role-play a conversation between another buyer and supplier. Use the language from *What do you say? 2*. Follow the instructions below.

– Student A: You are the buyer. You want to buy the things in the list below. Ask the supplier if he/she has them in stock.

– Student B: You are the supplier. Turn to page 101 to see what you have in stock. Ask the buyer how many of each item he/she wants.

2 Change roles and repeat the task.

– Student A: You are the supplier. Turn to page 97 to see what you have in stock. Ask the buyer how many of each item he/she wants.

– Student B: You are the buyer. Ask the supplier if he/she has the things in stock in the list below.

Buyer

You want to buy these things:

– One G500 Photo Printer

– Printer cartridges: 5 multi-colour cartridges

– Photo paper: 5 packs

– Bluetooth adapter

– Folders (for photos): 4

Objective: Place an order

1 **A buyer wants to buy some office supplies and telephones a supplier to place an order. Role-play the conversation. Follow the instructions below.**

- Take turns to be a buyer and a supplier. When you are the buyer, choose any items you want from the catalogue and be ready to tell your supplier what you want to order. When you are the supplier, ask the buyer what he/she would like to order and write down the number or quantity of each item.
- Take turns to speak. Follow the instructions below.
- Student A: You are the buyer. Turn to page 97 for your customer details.
- Student B: You are the supplier. Turn to page 101 for a list of prices.

Catalogue

☆☆☆☆☆
Five star trading company

Product	Product code
Envelopes	
White A4 (pack of 500)	EVWA4
White A5 (pack of 500)	EVWA5
Brown A4 (pack of 500)	EVBA4
Paper for photocopier	
White A4 (pack of 500 sheets)	CP804
White A3 (pack of 500 sheets)	CP803
Printer cartridges	
Black	GE490
Multi-colour	JA685
Desk diaries	
Executive	DDQ07
Standard	DDK07

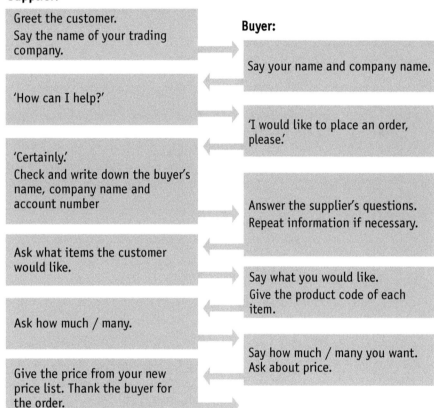

Supplier:

Greet the customer.
Say the name of your trading company.

'How can I help?'

'Certainly.'
Check and write down the buyer's name, company name and account number

Ask what items the customer would like.

Ask how much / many.

Give the price from your new price list. Thank the buyer for the order.

Buyer:

Say your name and company name.

'I would like to place an order, please.'

Answer the supplier's questions. Repeat information if necessary.

Say what you would like.
Give the product code of each item.

Say how much / many you want. Ask about price.

2 **Change roles and repeat the task.**

- Student A: You are the supplier. Turn to page 98 for a list of prices.
- Student B: You are the buyer. Turn to page 101 for your customer details.

Summary

In this unit, you have learnt to:

- ask about price and say prices correctly

- ask suppliers about stock

- place an order with a supplier

Writing 2 | Emails 2

| Write instructions | Request information | Place an order |

What do you write? 1

1 Read the email below in which Joe Di Marco tells Elena Stanislava how to get to his office. Complete the email with these words and phrases.

press   on the left   take the lift   say   take a taxi   use   go down

```
○○○                                                                    ⬭
 ⊘        💾       ⬅    ⬅⬅    ➡      🖨
Delete   Junk    Reply Reply All Forward  Print
         From:    Joe Di Marco
         To:      Elena Stanislava
         Subject: Project meeting

Dear Elena

I'm glad you can come to the meeting on Friday 14th. Here are some instructions to help you find
the way to my office:

¹_____ from the train station to 312 Torino Street. To enter the building, ²_____ the
entry phone near the door. ³_____ the button and wait for someone to answer.

⁴_____ your name and ask the receptionist to open the door.

Inside the building, ⁵_____ to the 4th floor. Turn left and ⁶_____ the corridor. My office is
the second door ⁷_____.

I look forward to seeing you on the 14th.
Best regards
Joe Di Marco
```

Task 1

Objective: Write instructions

Elena Stanislava is coming to your office (or another place you know). Write an email to her, giving some directions or instructions to help her find the way (from the train station or another place you choose). Write about five or six instructions.

What do you write? 2

Look at the advertisement for an electronic English dictionary. You are interested in it, but before you place an order, you need some information. Use one phrase from each column, A, B and C, to create five different requests or questions.

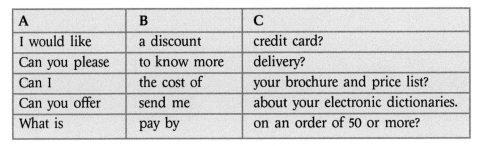

With this new electronic dictionary you can check your spelling and find the meaning of more than 250,000 English words and phrases.

A	B	C
I would like	a discount	credit card?
Can you please	to know more	delivery?
Can I	the cost of	your brochure and price list?
Can you offer	send me	about your electronic dictionaries.
What is	pay by	on an order of 50 or more?

Task 2

Objective: Request information

Write an email to Rightword Trading and ask for information about the electronic dictionary. You can use the phrases from the table on page 32, the phrases below, or any other phrases you like.

I am interested in ...   *Can you please ...?*

I look forward to hearing from you.   *Many thanks*

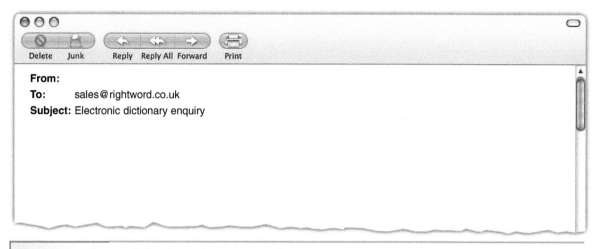

From:
To: sales@rightword.co.uk
Subject: Electronic dictionary enquiry

Task 3

Objective: Place an order

Write another email to Rightword Trading to place an order for some dictionaries. Combine the phrases below to create your email. Decide how to start and end the email.

My customer account number

50 Electronic European Language Dictionaries (product number EL770)

50 Electronic English dictionaries (product number EE415)

to place an order

to the address below.

is HG4459.

I would like

Please deliver

for the following items:-

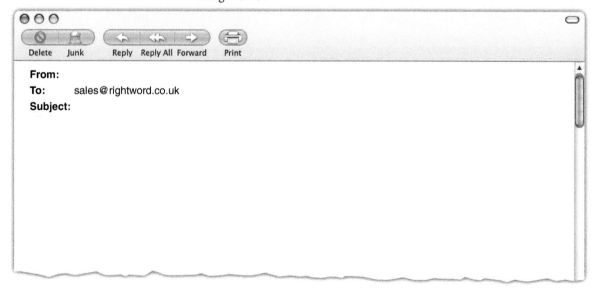

From:
To: sales@rightword.co.uk
Subject:

Unit 7 | Talk about projects

Warm up

When you want to buy something important, for example, a car, a PC, a camera, how do you decide what to buy? Do you ask people for recommendations, read about products in magazines or search the internet?

Building vocabulary

Verbs and nouns

Match the verbs on the left with the noun phrases on the right to describe some of the things you do before buying something. There is more than one way to match some of the verbs. Use a dictionary to help you.

go to   prices
telephone   a store
ask about   a decision
ask for   different suppliers
look at   recommendations
choose   the best model
make   different models

Past simple

1 How do you form the past simple of the verbs in *Building vocabulary*? Write the past simple of each verb in the correct column of the table.

+ -ed	+ -d	Irregular

2 What is the past simple of these verbs? Add them to the table.

arrive   meet   finish   spend   decide   start   work

 Grammar reference: Past simple affirmative, page 89

Task 1
Individually

Objective: Talk about past actions

Step 1 Preparation

Think of something you bought a short time ago. Where did you buy it? How did you choose it? Make a list of things you did before you bought it.

Whole class

Step 2 Practice

Say what you bought and explain where you bought it and how you chose it. Use the past simple.

Listening

1 Jack Delaney, the CEO of the Northern Bank, describes a project to buy new paintings for the bank's head office. Look at the list of actions below. In what sequence do you think he did them? Under *Your sequence*, order the actions 1–6.

Your sequence   Jack's sequence

☐   Visit different art galleries.   ☐
☐   Discuss the idea with the board of directors.   ☐
☐   Order the paintings.   ☐
☐   Set up a project team.   ☐
☐   Look at the finances and agree the budget.   ☐
☐   Present choices to the board.   ☐

CD 14 ⊙ **2** Listen to Jack Delaney and see if you were right. Write the correct number under *Jack's sequence*.

3 We often use the words and phrases below to show the sequence of actions. Jack Delaney uses some of these. Listen again and number them in the order that he uses them.

☐ First ...   ☐ After that ...   ☐ Finally ...
☐ Second ...   ☐ Then ... / So then ...
☐ Third ...   ☐ Next ...

Task 2
Pairs

Objective: Describe a project

Step 1 Practice

Practise describing the Northern Bank project: take turns to describe each action in the correct sequence. Start each one with an appropriate sequence word or phrase. Use the past simple.

Groups of 2-4

Step 2 Presentation

Choose one of the projects below, or think of a real project you have worked on. Imagine you were responsible for the project. What did you do? Write down five or six actions and number them to show the sequence. Then describe the project to the rest of your group using the past simple. You can start your talk like this:

I'd like to tell you about ...
The aim of the project was to ...

1   Finding a hotel for a conference
2   Arranging dinner at a restaurant for a group of important customers
3   Choosing new desks for your office

What do you say? 2 ## Talking about time

1 Read the details of the software project below and complete the sentences.

1   The first activity was to _____.
2   They _____ in July.
3   The project finished in _____.

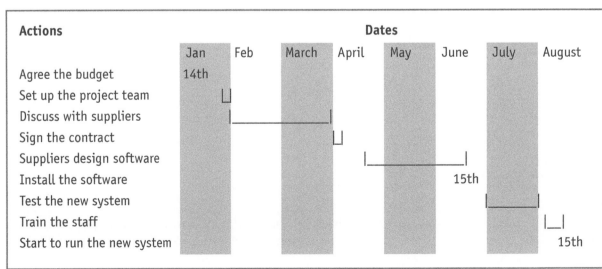

2 Read the sentences below about the project. Today is 16th August. Choose the correct time expression to complete each sentence.

in February and March   yesterday   between April and June
two months ago   last week   ~~on 14th January~~   at the end of January
at the beginning of April   last month

1   The Finance Department agreed the budget *on 14th January*.
2   We set up the project team _____.
3   The team discussed ideas for the new system with suppliers _____.
4   We signed a contract with the suppliers _____.
5   _____, the suppliers designed the new software.
6   They installed the software _____.
7   They tested the new system _____.
8   We trained the staff to use the new software _____.
9   We started to run the new system _____.

Strategies: Dates, page 77

Task 3
Pairs

Objective: Talk about time

1 Follow the instructions below.

–   Student A turn to page 98. You will see the details of a project that finished recently. Imagine you worked on this project and describe it to your partner. Say when each event happened: give the month or the precise date or say how long ago it happened.

–   Student B write the project title and complete the table below.

Project: _____

Actions	Dates				
	Aug	Sept	Oct	Nov	Dec

2 Change roles and repeat the task.

–   Student B turn to page 102.
–   Student A write the actions and dates in the table.

Summary

In this unit you have learnt to:

-   describe past actions

-   describe a project and give the sequence of actions

-   talk about time and say when you did something

Unit 8 | Solve problems

Warm up

Think of examples of electrical equipment that sometimes doesn't work. What kinds of problems with equipment do you sometimes have?

Building vocabulary

Using electrical equipment

1 Match these words with the pictures. Use a dictionary to help you.

connect   insert   plug in   turn on   press

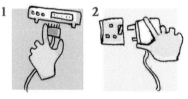

2 Look at the instructions to set up a DVD player and play a DVD. Number the instructions in the order that you could follow them.

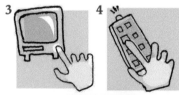

☐ Turn the TV on.
☐ Connect the DVD player to the TV.
☐ Press the <play> button.
☐ Plug the equipment in.
☐ Insert a DVD.
☐ Turn the DVD player on.

3 Describe the sequence to a partner. Use sequence words (*first, then, next*, etc.) and the imperative.

CD 15 ⊙ Listening 1

Rita da Silva is staying at a London hotel. She telephones the receptionist to complain about a problem. Listen to the conversation. What does Rita have a problem with?

a a lamp   b the television (TV)   c the shower   d the fridge

Describing a problem

Listen to the conversation again. Complete the sentences.

1 I have a _____ with the television.
2 I think there's something _____ with it.
3 I _____ turn it on.
4 I pressed the button but _____ happened.
5 It doesn't _____.
6 I think it's _____.

Strategies, Asking for help and being helpful, page 79

Task 1
Individually

Objective: Describe a problem

Step 1 Preparation

Imagine you are staying at a foreign hotel or conference centre. You have a problem with a piece of equipment. Think of a problem, e.g. there's no hot water and decide how you can describe it using the language from *What do you say? 1.*

Pairs

Step 2 Role-play

Take turns to be a guest with a problem and a receptionist. Role-play their telephone conversation. The guest should describe the problem and the receptionist should be helpful.

Asking check questions

When someone tells you about a problem, you often need to get more details so you can understand the problem. To find out more, it is useful to ask check questions.

Look at the procedure below to see how we make questions to check if someone followed the correct procedure. Write check questions for the other steps in the procedure. With a partner, practise asking and answering the questions.

Procedure to read email	Check questions	Answers
1 Plug the computer in.	What did you do first?	I plugged the computer in.
2 Turn the computer on.	Did you turn the computer on?	Yes, I did. / No, I didn't.
3 Wait for the computer to start up.		
4 Connect to the internet.		
5 Click on the email icon.		
6 Type your user name and password.		
7 Click on <check mail>.		

Grammar reference: Past simple negative, question and short answer, page 90

Task 2
Pairs

Objective: Ask check questions

1 Talk about problems. Follow the instructions.

- Student A choose a problem from the boxes below and describe it to your partner. If you can, make it a real problem (name a real person, document, etc.).
- Student B use the verbs in the list to ask check questions. Ask as many questions as you can think of.

What did you do?
Did you ...?

Problem 1	Problem 2	Problem 3	Problem 4
You can't contact someone, for example, a colleague or customer.	You can't find an important document.	You want to buy a ... but you can't find the one you want.	You want to find a word in English.
Check questions:	**Check questions:**	**Check questions:**	**Check questions:**
call his/her (mobile number / office)	leave it (near the photocopier)	look for suppliers (in the phone book)	go to WordReference.com
ask ...	look in ...	try ...	look in ...
send ...	ask ...	search ...	ask ...

2 Change roles and repeat the task.

CD 16 ⊙ Listening 2 **1 Steve is a computer technician in a small company. He helps other employees with their computer problems. Listen to a phone call between Steve and Fred Smith. Fred is an older employee who doesn't understand much about computers. Answer the questions.**

1 Does Fred have ...
   a a new computer?
   b an old computer?

2 What was his problem? He couldn't ...
   a turn it on.
   b connect to the internet.
   c check his email.

3 What did Fred see on the screen when he clicked on the email icon?
   a nothing
   b an error message
   c a box asking for his user name and password

4 What did Fred do next?

2 Steve explains the solution. Choose the correct words in *italics*. Listen again and check.

Well, that's why you *can't / couldn't* check your email. You *didn't / not* type your email address.

Task 3
Pairs

Objective: Explain the solution

Look at the problems and follow the instructions.

Problem 1

Setting up a digital projector to give a PowerPoint presentation

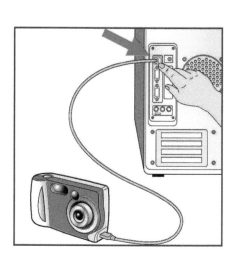

- Student A explain the problem: you tried to set up a PowerPoint presentation, but you couldn't get a picture on the screen. This is what you did:
  1. You plugged in the laptop and projector.
  2. You turned them on.
  3. You connected the laptop to the projector, as in the picture.

- Student B turn to page 104 to find the correct procedure. Ask check questions about each stage in the procedure to find out what your partner did or didn't do.

  What did you do first?

  What did you do next?

  Did you turn them on?

  After checking all the steps, tell your partner what they did or didn't do correctly.

Problem 2

Downloading photos from a digital camera to a computer

- Student B explain the problem: you tried to download photos from a camera, but you couldn't see the photos on your computer. This is what you did:
  1. You used the USB cable.
  2. You connected the camera to the computer's USB port.
  3. You clicked on the photo wizard.
  4. You followed the steps in the photo wizard.

- Student A turn to page 98 to find the correct procedure. Ask check questions about each stage in the procedure to find out what your partner did or didn't do.

  What did you do first?

  What did you do next?

  Did you turn the camera on?

  After checking all the steps, tell your partner what they did or didn't do correctly.

Summary

In this unit, you have learnt to:

- describe simple problems and ask for help
- ask check questions, for example, *What did you do?* and *Did you ...?*
- be helpful and explain solutions

Unit 9 | Describe products

| Warm up | What kind of car would you like to have? Give reasons. |

Building vocabulary

Adjectives

1 Choose the three best adjectives in the list to describe each type of car 1–3. Use a dictionary to help you. Think of other adjectives to describe the cars.

fast economical practical stylish strong safe reliable exciting easy (to park / drive)

2 Describe one of the cars using the adjectives above.

It's fast, it's exciting and it's very stylish.
This car is ..., ... and ... .
It's a ..., ... and ... car.

3 In small groups, choose three or four products you can describe. Then think of as many adjectives as you can to describe them. Choose something in the classroom, for example a mobile phone, a watch, an item of clothing. Or choose a well-known product and give the brand name.

4 Your trainer will write the names of each group's products on the board. Someone from each group should describe one product. Other groups try to guess which item you are describing.

 Grammar reference: Adjectives, page 91

Talking about size

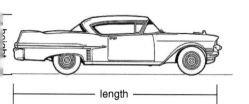

length

width

1 Look at the information and complete the sentences below with these words.

high   long   weighs   wide

1 The car is 5.070 metres _____.
2 It _____ 1,855 kilograms.
3 It is 1.950 metres _____.
4 It is 1.740 metres _____.

2 Take turns to ask and answer these questions.

1 How long is the car? / What is the length of the car?
2 How high is it? / What is its height?
3 How wide is it? / What is its width?
4 How heavy is it? / What does it weigh?

Task 1
Pairs

Objective: Talk about size

Look at the advert below for the KMX Sports Tricycle. At the back of the book, you can find the sizes of different models of the sports tricycle. Take turns to ask and answer questions about the sizes using the language from *What do you say? 1*. Write the sizes of each model in the table below.

- Student A, adult's sports tricycle, turn to page 98.
- Student B, child's sports tricycle, turn to page 100.

	Adult's sports tricycle	Child's sports tricycle
Height		
Length		
Width		
Weight		

Go anywhere
Fast, strong,
turns easily
High Performance sports tricycle
Fun for adults and chlidren

1 Brian Thorpe is a product manager with Magic, a company that manufactures products for the kitchen. Listen to Brian telling some customers about a new product, the Magic Egg Cooker. Does he talk about the size of the product?

2 Listen again and choose the correct option.

1 The Magic Egg Cooker cooks eggs   a with   b without water.
2 You can cook   a 2   b 4   c 6 eggs at the same time.
3 a You set the time.   b The cooker sets the time automatically.
4 The egg cooker is made of   a plastic   b rubber   c wood   d metal.
5 It is   a large and heavy   b small and light.
6 It cooks eggs   a slowly   b perfectly   c badly.

Grammar reference: Adverbs, page 91

| What do you say? 2 |

Describe a product

1 Match the phrases 1–5 with the phrases a–e to form five sentences that describe the product.

1 It's 20cm ...   a strong plastic.
2 You use it for ...   b long and 12 cm wide.
3 It's made of ...   c cooking eggs.
4 It's an ...   d cook eggs perfectly without any water.
5 You can ...   e egg cooker.

2 Which of the sentences 1–5 above answers each of these questions?

a What kind of product is it?   d Why is it special?
b What do you use it for?   e What size is it?
c What is it made of?

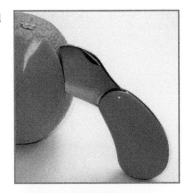

Task 2
Pairs

Objective: Describe products

1 Look at the products in the pictures on page 44. Go to the back of the book to find the details for products 1 and 2. Describe your product to your partner. Your partner should write down the details in the table below. Use the language from *What do you say?* 2.

- Student A describe product 1. Turn to page 98.
- Student B describe product 2. Turn to page 102.

	1	2	3	4
Product				
For ...?				
Made of ...?				
Size ...?				
Why special ...?				
Price				

2 With the same partner, take turns to ask and answer questions about products 3 and 4 and write the details in the table. You should only give the product information that your partner asks for.

Strategies: Talking about products, page 80

Task 3
Whole class

Objective: Say what you think

1 You all work for an online shop. Your job is to choose new products to sell on your website. Give your opinions about the sports tricycle, the egg cooker and the four products in *Task 2*.

I think it's a really good idea. / I don't think it's very useful.

I like it because you can carry it easily. / It's a good product but it's too expensive.

Individually

2 Think of a product you know about. Prepare a short description of it and then tell the rest of the class about it. Say why you like it. Say what you think about the products other people describe.

Summary

In this unit, you have learnt to:

- describe the size (length, width, height) of products
- describe the special features of products
- give your opinion of different products

Writing 3 | Report what you did

| Report on a trip | Report a problem |

1 Look at the schedule for a sales trip to Helsinki. With a partner, practise asking and answering questions about the schedule.

- Student A ask about Monday.
- Student B ask about Tuesday.

A: *When did you arrive in Helsinki?*

B: *I arrived on Monday at 10am.*

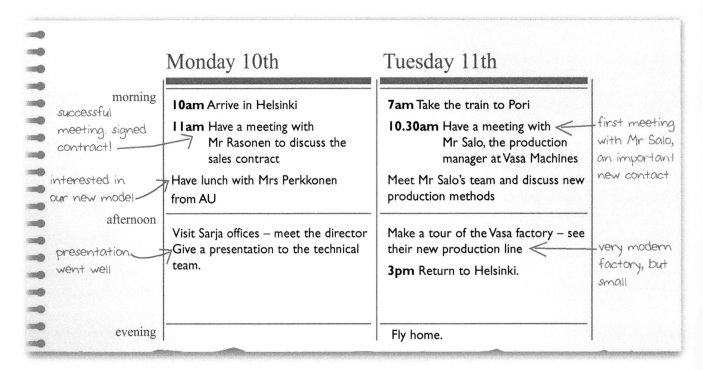

Monday 10th

morning

successful meeting: signed contract!

interested in our new model

10am Arrive in Helsinki

11am Have a meeting with Mr Rasonen to discuss the sales contract

Have lunch with Mrs Perkkonen from AU

afternoon

presentation went well

Visit Sarja offices – meet the director
Give a presentation to the technical team.

evening

Tuesday 11th

7am Take the train to Pori

10.30am Have a meeting with Mr Salo, the production manager at Vasa Machines

first meeting with Mr Salo, an important new contact

Meet Mr Salo's team and discuss new production methods

Make a tour of the Vasa factory – see their new production line

very modern factory, but small

3pm Return to Helsinki.

Fly home.

2 Put the sentences about Monday into the correct order according to when they happened (see the schedule above). The sentences make the first part of a report on the sales trip to Helsinki.

- [ ] She is interested in our new model.
- [ ] In the afternoon, we visited the Sarja offices and met the director.
- [1] We travelled to Helsinki on Monday, 10th and arrived at 10am.
- [ ] We gave a presentation to the technical team.
- [ ] It was a successful meeting: we signed the contract.
- [ ] We had a meeting with Mr Rasonen at 11am to discuss the sales contract.
- [ ] Then we had lunch with Mrs Perkkonen from AU.
- [ ] It went very well.

Task 1	**Objective: Report on a trip**

Now write the rest of the report on the sales trip to Helsinki (about Tuesday). Write a sentence for each event in the schedule using the past simple. Give the time of the event or use sequence words (*first, then, next, after that ...*) to show when it happened. Write another sentence for each of the notes.

What do you write? 2 Ahmed Yasin is a technician. He repairs equipment in the company where he works. After each problem, he writes a report for his boss in the technical department. Below is one of Ahmed's reports. Read the report and answer the questions.

Maintenance report

Name of engineer:	Ahmed Yasin
Date:	8th April
Details of problem:	There was a fault with a printer in the marketing department.
	The copies were black and there was a lot of ink inside the printer.
Reason:	One of the ink cartridges was broken.
Action:	I cleaned the printer and replaced the broken cartridge.
Result:	I tested the printer. It worked well.

1 Where was the problem?
2 Why was there a lot of ink inside the printer?
3 What did Ahmed do?
4 Did he fix the problem?

Task 2	**Objective: Report a problem**

Use the prompts to make sentences and put them in the correct parts of the report form below. You can write your own name and today's date.

1 paper / not go through / smoothly
2 fault / photocopier / finance department
3 paper tray / broken
4 test / photocopier
5 it / work / well
6 repair / paper tray

Maintenance report

Name of engineer:	
Date:	
Details of problem:	
Reason:	
Action:	
Result:	

Unit 10 | Talk about current activities

| Catch up with someone | Exchange news | Show someone round |

Warm up

What do you say in English when you greet people you know? What questions do you often ask? Which of the topics below do you usually ask about first?

- ☐ holidays / travel
- ☐ the other person's family
- ☐ health
- ☐ current activities

Building vocabulary

Activities

1 **Are you doing any of the activities below just now? Where possible, change the words in *italics* to make them true for you. What else are you doing? Use a dictionary to help you.**

I'm _____ at the moment / today / this week / this month.

... studying *French*.

... starting a project to *install a new software system*.

... doing some research on *the electronics market*.

... preparing for *a conference / an exhibition / an exam*

... planning a trip to *Australia*.

... designing a *new kind of product*.

... working on a *proposal for an important client*.

... writing a *marketing report*.

... applying for a new job in *marketing*.

2 Work with a partner. Talk about what you are doing at the moment, using the language on page 48. Then change partners and practise again. Respond to your partner's news, for example:

That sounds interesting / boring / difficult. Really?
That's good / bad. Oh, I'm glad / sorry to hear that.

Grammar reference: Present continuous, page 92

What do you say? 1

Catching up with someone you know

1 Complete the conversation with B's responses a–g.

A: Hello, Sylvia!

B: ¹_____

A: Fine thanks. How about you?

B: ²_____

A: What are you doing these days?

B: ³_____

A: Really? Are you enjoying it?

B: ⁴_____

A: I'm still with XLC. But I'm looking for a new job.

B: ⁵_____

A: I'm applying for jobs in advertising.

B: ⁶_____

A: It was good to see you again.

B: ⁷_____

A: Thanks. Bye.

a Yes, very much. What about you?

b Great!

c Good to see you, too. And good luck with the job applications!

d Well, best of luck! I'm afraid I can't stop – I'm late for an appointment.

e What kind of job?

f Hi, Ben. How are you?

g I'm working for AR Travel in the sales department.

2 Role-play the conversation with a partner.

Task 1
Pairs

Objective: Catch up with someone

You and your partner work for different companies. You last met two years ago at a conference in Milan. You are meeting now at a conference in Canada. Role-play your conversation, using the language from *What do you say? 1*. Make up information or talk about things you are doing in real life.

CD 18 ⊙ Listening 1   **1** Gerald Drake, the managing director of a subsidiary company, receives a visit from Regina Dumas, from head office. In the conversation, they talk about Miranda, who worked in Gerald's company in the past and is now working with Regina at head office. Listen to the conversation and answer the questions.

1 Regina asks: 'How's business?' Is Gerald's business doing well or badly?

2 Gerald's company has a new model. Where are they planning to launch it?

2 Listen again and answer the questions.

1 Regina asks Gerald: 'How are you?' What does he respond?
2 What are Gerald's salespeople working on at the moment?
3 What does Regina say when she hears about this?
4 Gerald asks about Miranda. What is Miranda doing now?
5 Gerald wants to send greetings to Miranda. What does he say?
6 How does Regina reply?

What do you say? 2 ## Asking about someone else

1 Use the phrases below to make two different conversations of four lines each. Both conversations start with questions.

How's Alex? Is he still travelling a lot?

I will.

How are Tony and Lisa? Are they still working in the finance office?

No, he isn't travelling much now.

Well, give him my regards.

Certainly.

Yes, they are.

Well, give them my regards.

2 Practise the two conversations with a partner.

Task 2
Pairs

Objective: Exchange news

You and your partner worked together in the past, but now one of you has a new job. You meet at a conference. Role-play your conversation.

– Student A follow the instructions below for part 1.
– Student B turn to page 102 and follow the instructions for part 1.
– Then follow the instructions for part 2 (Student A below and Student B on page 102).

Part 1
– Greet your partner. Ask how he/she is.
– Ask: How is your new job?
– Answer your partner's question about Frank: working in China; helping to start a new factory there.
– Answer your partner's question about Darlene and Federico: planning to get married; looking for a place to live.

Part 2
– Greet your partner. Ask how he/she is.
– Answer your partner's question: You are enjoying the new job; working with interesting people, making new contacts.
– Ask about Stella.
– Ask about Carlos and Ugo.
– Send greetings to them.

 Strategies: Meeting people you know, page 76

1 William Trim is showing Una Small round his coffee processing plant. Below are the three parts of the tour. Listen to the conversation. Number the places in the order that Una visits them.

☐ processing section   ☐ quality control   ☐ warehouse

2 What usually happens in each place? Match the activities with the places in exercise 1.

a They store the coffee beans.   b They taste the coffee.

c They roast and grind the beans.

3 Listen again. What is happening in each place? Complete the activities with the present continuous of the verb in brackets. Then write the place where each activity is happening.

		Place
1	Martina _____ (prepare) cups of coffee.	*quality control*
2	The truck _____ (deliver) supplies.	_____
3	Joe _____ (check) the colour of the beans.	_____
4	Alicia _____ (try) to repair the machine.	_____
5	Bruno _____ (taste) the coffee.	_____
6	The machine _____ (not work).	_____

4 Look at the picture of the stick people on the right. Which part of the tour does it show?

Task 3
Pairs

Objective: Show someone round

1 Role-play the tour of the coffee processing plant with your partner. Follow the steps below.

1 Introduce each place:
   This is the ...

2 Say what you usually do in each place, for example:
   We store the beans here.

3 Describe what is happening now and what the workers are doing.

Pairs or
small groups

2 Draw three or four simple pictures showing different parts of the office or factory where you work, or the college where you study. Draw one or two stick people working in each place. Imagine you are showing someone round and explain what each place is. Describe what is happening and what the people are doing.

Summary

In this unit, you have learnt to:

- greet people you know and talk about what you are doing

- exchange news of other people

- show someone round the place where you work and describe what is happening

Unit 11 | Compare and discuss

| Give your opinion | Make comparisons | Choose the best |

Warm up

Where do you usually stay when you travel? What do you look for when you choose a place to stay? What kind of hotel do you like?

What do you say? 1

Giving opinions

Match the headings 1–5 with the phrases a–h below.

1 Ask someone for their opinion (2 answers)
2 Introduce your opinion (2 answers)
3 Give a negative opinion (2 answers)
4 Say something positive and something negative (1 answer)
5 Give a reason for your opinion (1 answer)

a In my opinion ...
b I like it / I don't like it because ...
c What do you think (of) ...?
d What's your opinion (of) ...?

e I think ... / I don't think ...
f It's very nice, but it isn't cheap.
g It isn't big enough.
h I think it's too (expensive, far from the airport).

 Strategies: Discussing ideas, page 80

Task 1	Objective: Give your opinion
Pairs	

Step 1 Description

You and your partner often visit Amsterdam on business but you usually stay at different hotels (your company arranges the hotel for you). Read the description of your hotel. Tell your partner about your hotel.

- Student A look at the information about Hotel Guilder.
- Student B turn to page 103 and look at the information about Hotel Waterside.

Hotel Guilder

A small hotel in an old building in the city centre, three stars

18 rooms

No restaurant in the hotel

Near the shopping centre, restaurants and places of interest

Lots of things to do in the evening

Your room: noisy, not big enough

Price for the room: €90 (not expensive)

I usually stay at ...
It's ...
It has ...

Step 2 Discussion

Give your opinion about your hotel and the reasons why you like it or don't like it. Use the language from *What do you say?* 1. Ask your partner about his/her hotel. What is his/her opinion of it?

What do you say? 2	**Making comparisons**

1 The sentences below compare the Hotel Waterside with the Hotel Guilder. Work with a partner. Complete the sentences with the correct adjectives in *italics*.

1 The Waterside is *larger / smaller* than the Guilder.
2 The Guilder is *more modern / older* than the Waterside.
3 The Waterside is *more expensive / cheaper* than the Guilder.
4 The Guilder is *nearer to / further from* the city centre.
5 The rooms at the Guilder are *quieter / noisier*.
6 The rooms at the Waterside are *better / worse* because they are large and quiet.
7 It's *easier / more difficult* to visit the city centre when you stay at the Waterside.

2 Which hotel do you prefer? Why?

 Grammar reference: Comparatives, page 93

Task 2
Pairs

Objective: Make comparisons

Step 1 Preparation

1 Your team is responsible for planning an important conference. There are two possible locations for the conference: Read the information about Durban and Budapest and answer the questions.

1 Which city is better for water sports?
2 Which city is better for cultural activities?

Durban

Durban (population 3.7 million): A lively city by the sea. It has excellent beaches and is a good place for water sports. The climate is very warm (21 to 30°C). The city is modern with good transport. Restaurants serve African, Asian and European food. Near to Durban, you can go on a safari or go mountain climbing. Living costs are very low.

BUDAPEST   HUNGARY

Budapest (population 2 million): A beautiful, historic city on the river Danube. It has many interesting buildings and is a good place to enjoy music and nightlife. The climate is cold in winter and warm in summer (-1 to 22° C).

The city has good transport. There are some very good restaurants (Hungarian and international food). You can visit the thermal baths and swim in warm pools all year round. Living costs are quite low.

2 With your partner, compare the two cities. Then write one or two sentences about each of the topics below using the adjectives in brackets in the comparative form as in *What do you say? 1.*

- population (big / small)
- general description (modern, beautiful)
- climate (warm / cold)
- living costs (low / high)
- distance (near to / far from your home town or company's head office)

Groups of
2–4

Step 2 Discussion

Say which city you think is better for your conference and give reasons for your opinion. Do you all agree?

Building vocabulary

Conference centres

Match the phrases with the definitions. Use a dictionary to help you.

1 conference facilities   **a** rooms where people can sleep

2 air conditioning   **b** a large area where you can display things (e.g. products)

3 accommodation

4 exhibition space   **c** a system that makes the air cooler

5 leisure facilities   **d** rooms, equipment and services for conferences

6 latest technology   **e** the newest, most modern equipment

   f places for different free-time activities (e.g. swimming pool, tennis courts, gym)

CD 20 ⊙ Listening **Part 1**

Nico, Pauline and Jacques work for Lawton Corporation. They are planning a conference. Listen to the first part of their discussion and answer the questions.

1 How many people usually come to the conference?

2 How much exhibition space do they need?

CD 21 ⊙ **Part 2**

Listen to the second part of the discussion. Look at the list and tick (✓) the things they talk about. Which one do they think is the most important for choosing a conference centre?

☐ air conditioning   ☐ low costs

☐ a location near the airport   ☐ good restaurants

☐ equipment with the latest technology   ☐ leisure facilities

Grammar reference: Superlatives, page 93

Task 3
Groups of
2 or 3

Objective: Choose the best

Step 1 Exchange information

You each have information at the back of the book about one conference centre. Ask questions about the other two centres and write down the information your partner(s) give you in the table below. Answer your partners' questions about your conference centre.

– Student A turn to page 99.

– Student B turn to page 102.

– Student C turn to page 103.

	Centre A: Durban	**Centre B: Budapest**	**Centre C: Tokyo**
Accommodation			
Space for exhibitions			
Distance from airport			
Special feature			
Cost			

Step 2 Discussion

Refer back to the list in *Listening part 2*. Look at the table and discuss the points below. Then give your opinions about which centre is best for Lawton Corporation.

– Which centre is the biggest / smallest / cheapest / most expensive?

– Which centre is the best size for the number of people?

– Which centre is the nearest to the airport / easiest to get to?

– Which is the best for: a) technology b) food c) leisure facilities?

Summary

In this unit, you have learnt to:

- ask for and give opinions

- make comparisons

- discuss which is the best

Unit 12 | Interview for a job

| Ask about experience | Describe your career | Do a job interview |

Warm up

Talk about your most exciting experience. For example, was it: driving a fast car, meeting a famous person, going to a pop concert, mountain climbing or something else?

What do you say? 1

Have you ever ...?

Work with a partner. Ask and answer questions about your experiences. Use these ideas and any others you can think of.

- *driven* a Ferrari / a bus / an electric car ...?
- *met* a film star / a TV star ...?
- *been* to the US / a world cup football match ...?
- *been* skiing / sailing / mountain climbing ...?
- *seen* the Pyramids / the Great Wall of China ...?

Have you ever driven a Ferrari? Yes, I have. or *No, I haven't. / No, never.*

 Grammar reference: Present perfect, page 94

Task 1
Pairs

Objective: **Ask about work experience**

Ask questions with *Have you ever ...?* to find out about your partner's work experience. Answer with *Yes, I have* or *No, I haven't* and add any details you like. Use these ideas.

travel on business   change jobs

work in sales / marketing / finance / administration

be responsible for a team / a department

do something that was very difficult

1 Listen to Matt Flinders describing his career and his life. Answer the questions.

1 Has Matt ever worked in a foreign country?
2 What is Matt's job now?

2 Listen again and complete the text with the correct date or number of years.

From 1995 to ¹_____, Matt studied business administration at university. His first job was with Smartex, a retail company based in the UK. In ²_____, Matt joined Market World, an international retail company. After ³_____ years there, Market World offered Matt a job as a manager in a new store in Indonesia.

Matt moved back to the UK in November ⁴_____. He stayed with Market World and worked as the general manager in a Liverpool store. In June ⁵_____ Matt got married. Market World promoted Matt to be the regional manager in October ⁶_____.

3 Use the text above to answer these questions about Matt's career. Answer with a complete sentence and use the correct tense: present perfect or past simple. Use *since* + year or *for* + number of years.

1 How long did Matt study at university?
2 How long did he work in Indonesia?
3 How long did he work as the general manager in Liverpool?
4 How long has he been married?
5 How long has he been the regional manager?

 Grammar reference: *for* and *since*, page 94

Describing a career

Find out about a person's career and use the information to complete the sentences below.

– Student A turn to page 99.
– Student B turn to page 103.

1 I studied at ... University / College from ... to ... .
2 I have a degree / a qualification in ... .
3 My first job was with ... [organisation].
4 I worked in ... (the ... department) / as a/an ... [job title].
5 Then I left ... [organisation] and joined ... [organisation].
6 I stayed there for ... years.
7 After that I studied for ... at ... .
8 Then I got a job as ... .
9 I'm still ... .
10 I've worked in ... [job area, e.g. retailing] for ... years.

Task 2

Objective: Describe your career

1 Role-play the conversation.

– Student A: Play the role of Hei Ping Tan. Tell your partner about your career. Use the language from *What do you say? 2*.

– Student B: Your partner will give you information to complete the table below. Ask questions to check, e.g. *Where was that? When did you start / finish that job? Sorry, can you repeat the date, please?*

		Date
University / College		
Qualification		
First job		
Second job		
Second qualification		
Current job		

2 Change roles. Ask and answer questions about Claude Naudet.

– Student B: Play the role of Claude Naudet. Tell your partner about your career.

– Student A: Complete the table above with the information your partner gives you.

3 Take turns to ask questions and give details about your real career or education.

Building vocabulary **Job advertisements**

Operations Manager
At John F Kennedy airport, New York

Air Germanica is looking for a well-organised person with good people skills to manage its airport operations in New York. This is a very good opportunity for someone who wants to develop their career in the airline industry.

Requirements: Candidates must have a degree and at least four years' experience working in airline operations. Must speak English and German. Excellent salary and travel benefits.

Look at the advertisement and match the circled phrases with the definitions below. Use a dictionary to help you.

1 people who apply for a job: _____
2 money that a company pays monthly to its employees: _____
3 can work well with other people: _____
4 free or low-cost travel for the employee: _____
5 someone who can do things efficiently: _____
6 what the company wants or expects from the people who apply: _____

CD 23 ⊙ Listening 2 **1 Inga Muller is applying for the job in the advertisement above. She has an interview with Ken Starr. Listen and number the interviewer's questions in the order that you hear them.**

☐ Why do you want this job?
☐ What do you want to do in the future?
☐ Have you been responsible for a team of people before?
☑ Can you tell me a bit about yourself?
☐ How long have you worked in the airline industry?
☐ Have you ever lived in a foreign country?
☐ What special skills do you have?

Listen again. Are these statements true or false? Correct the false statements.

1 Inga Muller studied Business Administration.
2 She has worked in the airline industry for two years.
3 At present, she is an operations manager with Hi-Fly.
4 She wants to work for a small airline.
5 She has never lived abroad before.
6 She speaks two languages.
7 She doesn't have any plans for the future.

Strategies: Asking questions, page 81

Task 3

Objective: Do a job interview

A big travel company that sells holidays in Europe and the US is looking for someone to develop new holiday ideas. The job includes travel to different countries and making contacts with people. The company hopes to find someone who:

- wants a career in the travel industry
- has worked in the travel industry for five years or more
- has worked in a sales team
- has good IT skills
- speaks English and one other European language
- has travelled a lot, especially in Europe or the US

Pairs

Step 1 Role-play

Take turns to play the roles of interviewer and candidate for the job above.

- The interviewer: You should ask the questions from *Listening 2* exercise 1. You can ask any other questions you like to get more information.
- The candidate: You should use your own name and nationality.
- Student A: When you are the candidate, turn to page 99.
- Student B: When you are the candidate, turn to page 100.

Groups of up to 6

Step 2 Discussion

Discuss the information you got about each candidate with the rest of your group. Which person would you employ? Why?

Summary

In this unit you have learnt to:
- talk and ask questions about experience
- describe your career
- ask and answer interview questions

Writing 4 | Letters

What do you write? 1

1 Match the situations with the opening and then the closing greetings.

	Situation	Opening	Closing
1	Letter to a company – you don't know the name of the person who will read it	a Dear Mr Hendrix	d Kind regards / Best wishes
2	Business letter – you know the name of the person who will read it	b Dear John	e Yours sincerely
3	Informal letter to a friend or colleague	c Dear Sir or Madam	f Yours faithfully

2 Look at the letter on the left below. What kind of letter is it? Use the information in *What do you write? 1* to help you. Then find and <u>underline</u> the following.

1 the name of the writer   2 the address he wrote to

3 the date of the letter   4 the subject line

Reservations Manager
Arrow Bank Hotel
Midford

12th September, 20

Dear Sir or Madam

Re: Reservation enquiry

I would like to reserve four single rooms and one double room for three nights, from 1st to 4th November. We would like room and breakfast only.

Could you please confirm your current prices?

I look forward to hearing from you.

Yours faithfully

James Lees

James Lees

---

[1] *Dear Mr Lees / Hi James*

[2] *Good to hear from you. / Thank you for your enquiry.*

[3] *I am pleased to confirm your reservation for / It's OK for you to have* four single rooms and one double room from the first to the fourth of November. The price for the single rooms is €95; the price for the double room is €135, room and breakfast only.

[4] *Please let me know if you have any questions or special requests. / Tell me if you need anything else.*

[5] *See you in November. / We look forward to welcoming you at our hotel.*

[6] *Best regards / Yours sincerely*

G. Donatelli

Giorgio Donatelli, Reservations Manager

---

3 <u>Underline</u> the best phrases in *italics* in the Reservation Manager's reply on the right above. Why did you choose each phrase? Could you use the other phrases in a different kind of letter?

Task 1

Objective: Reserve hotel rooms

You and three colleagues would like to stay at the Classica Hotel. Write a letter to the reservations manager to make the reservation. Use the information below.

- You would like to stay from 9th to 19th April.
- You would like single rooms with breakfast and dinner.
- You are travelling by car from the airport. Ask the manager to send you some directions.

What do you write? 2

1 Look at the job advertisement and answer the questions.

1 What is the job?
2 What qualifications do candidates need to have?
3 Do candidates need to have any special experience?
4 What skills do they need?

Positiva Pharmaceuticals

Positiva Pharmaceuticals requires an experienced sales representative to join their expanding sales team. Candidates must have:

- A degree in science
- Sales or marketing diploma
- Three years or more working in sales
- Excellent IT skills

Experience of the pharmaceuticals industry is an advantage

Apply in writing to Mr M Knight, Positiva Pharmaceuticals, PO Box 42, Newtown NT4100

Please quote Job Reference no: DEF 39

Task 2

Objective: Apply for a job

Look at the career details for Davina Lawrence. Davina wants to apply for the job in the advertisement. Write her letter of application using the information below.

Qualifications:	Degree in biology (2004); Diploma in marketing from Excel Business School (2007)
Work experience:	Sales representative for a food company (2004–6); Sales representative for Westons, a small pharmaceuticals company (since 2007). In present job: work in a team; specialise in sales of vitamins; helped to increase sales by 20 per cent last year.
Special skills:	IT and website design.

Optional task

Write a short letter of application for a job you would like. Use your own career details. (Or you can invent the details if you like).

Unit 13 | Suggest ideas

| Give advice and make suggestions | Brainstorm ideas | Hold a meeting |

Warm up

How do you solve your problems?

- Do you discuss them with other people or do you solve them on your own?
- Which people do you sometimes ask for suggestions or advice?
- Why is it a good idea to discuss things with other people?

What do you say? 1

Advice and suggestions

1 Look at the problem and complete sentences 1 and 2. Choose the words in *italics* which you think are best.

> **Problem**
> I have an important meeting today, but I have flu and I feel terrible. Should I go to the meeting or stay at home?

1   You *should / shouldn't* stay at home. You need to get well and you don't want to give your flu to other people.

2   You *should / shouldn't* stay at home. The meeting is important.

2 Look at the problem and the possible solutions. Decide if each sentence 1–4 is advice (a strong recommendation) or a suggestion (a possible action).

> **Problem**
> A friend has offered me a ticket for an international football match. But the match is on a work day. I really want to go. What should I do? Should I tell my manager that I have flu and then go to the match?

1 You *should* tell your friend that you can't go because you're working.
2 You *could* ask your manager for a day off.
3 You *shouldn't* tell your manager that you have flu.
4 *Perhaps / Maybe* you *could* sell the ticket to someone else.

 Grammar reference: Modal verbs *could* and *should*, page 95

Task 1
Pairs or small groups

Objective: Give advice and make suggestions

For each of the problems below, one person should explain the problem and ask for advice. The other(s) should give advice or make suggestions using the language from *What do you say? 1*.

> **Problem 1**
> I have a shop in the city centre and I sell food products: fruit, vegetables, sweets, drinks, etc. We open at 9.00am and close at 5.30pm, but I want to keep the shop open till 6.30 or 7.00 in the evening because many workers want to shop after 5.30 or 6pm. I employ three staff in the shop. They are very good staff, but they don't want to work longer hours. What should I do?

> **Problem 2**
> I have a small hotel in the city centre. There aren't many guests and I'm losing money. I don't have a website and guests can't book via the internet. My prices are a little higher than other hotels in the area, but I offer something special: I have pretty rooms which are all painted pink; I put fresh flowers in the rooms every day and I offer my guests free drinks. What else could I do to bring in more guests?

Brainstorming ideas

What do you say? 2

1 More and more people at Hard Graft Inc. are taking sick leave. The company wants to improve the health and fitness of its employees. The managers have asked each team to brainstorm some ideas. Combine the phrases for brainstorming 1–6 with the ideas a–c to make complete sentences.

1 We could ...
2 I think we should ...
3 Perhaps we could ...
4 Why don't we ...
5 Let's ...
6 How about ...

a arrange fitness classes every morning?
b invite a health consultant to come and give a talk.
c having more healthy food in the company restaurant?

2 Which of the responses a–h below show that 1) you agree with the suggestion, 2) you don't agree or 3) you are not certain or don't completely agree?

a ☐ I don't think that's a good idea because ...

b ☐ I agree.

c ☐ That's a good idea.

d ☐ I don't agree.

e ☐ I'm not sure.

f ☐ I like that idea.

g ☐ Yes, but ...

h ☐ You're right.

3 Work with a partner. Use the responses above to say what you think of the ideas in exercise 1. Suggest other ideas to improve the health and fitness of employees. Respond to them, with reasons if possible.

Task 2
Groups of 3 or 4

Objective: Brainstorm ideas

You all work together in the same team. Choose one of the problems below and brainstorm some ideas. Use the language from *What do you say?* 2. Be ready to report your ideas to the rest of the class.

1 Your manager wants to help you work together and solve problems more efficiently. She has asked you to suggest some ideas for a weekend of team-building activities, for example, go sailing, go on a camping trip.

2 A woman in your team is retiring after 35 years in the company. You have €150 to spend on a gift and/or a party for her. How could you spend the money?

3 Your team has moved to a different office in an old building. It is dark and unfriendly. Think of some ideas for making the room brighter and more cheerful.

Building vocabulary | **Verbs and nouns**

We can say *suggest* or *make a suggestion*. Complete the phrases with the appropriate verb: *give, make, do* or *hold*.

1 arrange: _____ an arrangement

2 work: _____ some work

3 decide: _____ a decision

4 meet: _____ a meeting

5 advise: _____ some advice

6 shop: _____ some shopping

CD 24 ⊙ Listening | **1** A team at Hard Graft Inc. are holding a meeting. They want to help people in the office to stop smoking. They discuss several ideas. Choi is the team leader. He starts the meeting and asks for ideas. The other people (in order of speaking) are: Sam, Pippa and Justine. Listen to the discussion and answer the questions.

1 Who makes the suggestion to close the smoking room – Justine, Pippa or Sam?

2 Who should find out about the cost of courses – Justine, Pippa or Sam?

Listen again. Choi uses several phrases to introduce the meeting, to ask for ideas and to request action. Number these phrases in the order that you hear them.

a ☐ Sam, what do you think?   d ☐ Welcome to the meeting, everyone.

b ☐ Justine, would you like to ...? e ☐ Any other ideas?

c ☐ As you know, ...

3 Which of the phrases a–e above does Choi use to do the following?

1 ☐ Start the meeting.   4 ☐ Ask someone to do something.

2 ☐ Introduce the problem.   5 ☐ Ask a team member for an

3 ☐ Ask the group for more ideas.   opinion.

Strategies: Meetings, page 81

Task 3
Groups of
3–5

Objective: Hold a meeting

Step 1 Preparation

1 Your group works as a team at Hard Graft Inc. You want to find ways to help employees to reduce stress. Choose *one* of the ideas below but don't discuss it yet.

– Set up a games room with table tennis and billiards (or other activities).

– Play music in the office (radio or music CDs).

– Start a sports club or a social club (discuss what kind of club).

– Your idea: _____

2 Choose a role for each person in the group. Each person should then prepare what they want to say.

– Student A: You lead the meeting.

– Student B: You agree with the idea.

– Student C: You don't agree with the idea.

– Student D: You can choose to agree or disagree.

Step 2 Role-play

Hold the meeting. Use the language from *Strategies*. Change roles and hold another meeting with a different idea from the list above.

Summary

In this unit, you have learnt to:

- give advice and make suggestions

- brainstorm ideas and respond to ideas

- lead a meeting and take part in a meeting

Unit 14 | Make arrangements

| Describe plans | Make phone calls | Arrange to meet |

Warm up

Do you plan your future activities in detail? Or do you make decisions to do things at the last minute? Do you make lists of things to do? Do you use a diary / calendar / schedule?

Task 1
Pairs

Objective: Describe a plan

1 Describe some travel plans. Follow the instructions below.

- Student A: You and your team are flying to Mexico next week. Another team member has made the plan for the trip. Find out about the plan and write the information in the schedule below.
- Student B: Turn to page 103 and use the information to answer your partner's questions.

Note: When we have made a definite arrangement for the future, we use the present continuous to talk about it.

What are we doing on Monday?

We're flying to Mexico City. We're leaving at ...

	Monday	Tuesday	Wednesday	Thursday	Friday	Weekend
am						
pm						

2 **Change roles and practise again.**

- Student B: Some important clients from Canada are visiting your office. Ask your partner about the plan and complete the schedule on page 66.
- Student A: Turn to page 99 and use the information to answer your partner's questions.

 Grammar reference: Present continuous for future, page 96

CD 25 ⊙ Listening 1

1 **Listen to a phone call and answer the questions.**

1   Why can't Jane Kelly speak to David Potts?
2   Who can she speak to?
3   What does Paul agree to do?
   a   arrange a meeting with David
   b   ask David to call Jane
   c   call Jane this afternoon

2 **Listen again and complete the telephone message which Paul leaves for David Potts.**

> TELEPHONE MESSAGE FOR: David
> MESSAGE:
> Jane Kelly from Greenshanks called this
> morning. She has some ¹ _____ for
> the new brochure to show you. She would
> like to ² _____ a ³ _____ with
> you. Please call her back before ⁴
> _____ . Her number is: ⁵ _____
>
> CALL TAKEN BY: Paul

What do you say? 1 **Get through to someone on the telephone**

Match the functions 1–6 with the phrases a–f.

1   Ask to speak to someone:
2   Give the reason for the call.
3   Ask someone to wait.
4   Introduce yourself when you are the caller.
5   Offer to take a message.
6   Ask for someone's number.

a   Just a moment, please.
b   This is Jane Kelly from Greenshanks.
c   Can you give me your number?
d   Can I speak to David Potts, please?
e   Can I take a message?
f   I'm calling about your new brochure.

 Strategies: Telephoning, page 82

Telephoning

Below are some other phrases you could hear on the telephone. Complete the phrases with these words.

available   calling   hold   leave   through

1   Ask someone to wait: _____ the line, please.

2   Ask for the caller's name: Who's _____, please?

3   Tell the caller you will connect them to a person or department: I'll put you _____.

4   Tell the caller that someone isn't there: I'm afraid Mr Tew isn't _____ just now.

5   Offer to take a message: Would you like to _____ a message?

Task 2
Pairs

Objective: Make phone calls

Step 1 Practice

Practise this telephone call with your partner. Take turns to be the person answering the phone and the caller. Follow the instructions.

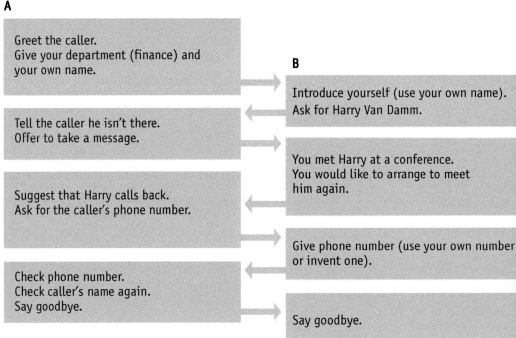

A

Greet the caller.
Give your department (finance) and your own name.

B

Introduce yourself (use your own name).
Ask for Harry Van Damm.

Tell the caller he isn't there.
Offer to take a message.

You met Harry at a conference.
You would like to arrange to meet him again.

Suggest that Harry calls back.
Ask for the caller's phone number.

Give phone number (use your own number or invent one).

Check phone number.
Check caller's name again.
Say goodbye.

Say goodbye.

Step 2 Role-play

Practise these telephone calls with your partner.

Call 1

–   Student A: You call the technical department to speak to Terry Lamark. Terry isn't in the office. Turn to page 102.

–   Student B: You are Terry's colleague. Answer the phone, find out who is calling and take a message.

Call 2

–   Student B: You call the personnel department to speak to Monika Diski. Monika isn't in the office. Turn to page 104.

–   Student A: You are Monika's colleague. Answer the phone, find out who is calling and take a message.

David Potts calls Jane Kelly to arrange a meeting. Listen to the conversation and answer the questions.

1 Where do they plan to meet?
2 Can David meet Jane tomorrow? Why? / Why not?
3 Is Jane free next Monday? Why? / Why not?
4 What day and time do they agree to meet?

What do you say? 2

Arranging to meet

Number the sentences in the correct order, 1–8, to complete the conversation.

– **A:** I'd like to discuss the Morocco project. Can we meet?
– **B:** OK. What's a good day for you?

A

☐ I'm afraid I'm going to London on Tuesday. How about Friday?

☐ That's good for me.

☐ Monday's good. Are you free then?

☐ How about 8 o'clock?

B

☐ I'm sorry, I can't make 8 o'clock. We could meet at 8.30.

☐ OK then. I'll see you Friday at 8.30.

☐ Friday's fine. What time?

☐ I'm sorry, I'm very busy on Monday. How about Tuesday?

Task 3
Pairs

Objective: Arrange to meet

1 You and your partner work in different cities. Role-play a telephone conversation in which you arrange a day and time to meet. Follow the instructions below.

– Student A: You would like to visit Student B in their office next week. You need two to three hours for the meeting and one hour (each way) for your journey. You make the call. Turn to page 104.
– Student B: You answer the call. Use the schedule below.

	Monday	Tuesday	Wednesday	Thursday	Friday
am	10–11am Meeting with finance manager 11.30 Visit suppliers (stay for lunch)		Important client visit (all day)		9am–12.30 Management team meeting
pm				4.30pm International conference call (one hour)	

2 Draw up your own schedules for next week. Write at least three arrangements in the schedule. Then arrange another meeting with your partner.

Summary

In this unit, you have learnt to:

- describe plans and talk about definite arrangements in the future

- make phone calls, ask to speak to someone, and give and take messages

- arrange a meeting

Unit 15 | Predict future trends

| Make predictions | Talk about trends | Present a graph |

Warm up

Which of the following do you expect to see in the next 20 years? Why? / Why not?

- Smaller computers
- More jobs
- A lower retirement age
- Cheaper air travel

Building vocabulary

Trends

1 Match the words and phrases 1–3 with the phrases a–c that mean the same.

1 increase   a stay the same
2 decrease   b go up
3 remain steady   c go down

2 Use the verbs above to make predictions about each of the following topics.

- The world's population   - The population of your country
- Oil supplies   - The price of mobile phones

The world's population will increase.

3 Make predictions about other things that will increase or decrease in the future.

 Grammar reference: *will*, page 96

Certain or possible?

How certain are you about the predictions you have made? Match the phrases in **bold** in sentences 1–8 with a–d.

1 I'm **certain that** computers will be much smaller.
2 It's **unlikely that** the price of petrol will fall.
3 **Perhaps** there'll be no unemployment.
4 It's **likely that** people will live longer.
5 We **probably won't** work less.
6 House prices **will probably** rise.
7 **We'll definitely** have better medical care.
8 **Maybe** we will all drive electric cars.

a certainty
b probability
c possibility
d improbability

Task 1
Groups of
3 or 4

Objective: Make predictions

Look at the predictions below. Do you think they are they certain, probable, possible or improbable? Tell the rest of your group what you think. Use the phrases from *What do you say? 1.*

1 We'll download all our books from the internet.
2 Handwriting will disappear and we won't need to use pens.
3 Space travel will be cheaper and more people will become space tourists.
4 There will be a higher percentage of women CEOs in business.
5 Cities will be very quiet places because there won't be any cars.
6 One day, everyone in the world will speak English and there won't be any other languages.

CD 27 ⊙ **Listening 1**

Part 1

Lee Kuan Dok's TV manufacturing company has developed a new technology which gives very high quality pictures (HQV). Lee is giving a presentation about the future of the new TVs. Listen to the beginning of the presentation and number these things in the order that he says he will talk about them.

☐ Sales ☐ Price trend ☐ Market

CD 28 ⊙ **Part 2**

Listen to the rest of Lee's presentation. Match the information 1–3 with the graphs a–c.

1 the market for HQV TVs in the next five years
2 sales of the company's first HQV model
3 the price trend for HQV TVs

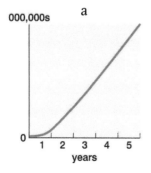

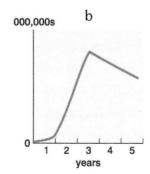

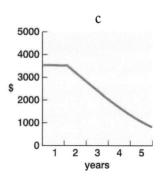

Describing graphs

1 Label the graphs below with these descriptions.

go down   increase slowly   remain steady   increase quickly   reach a peak

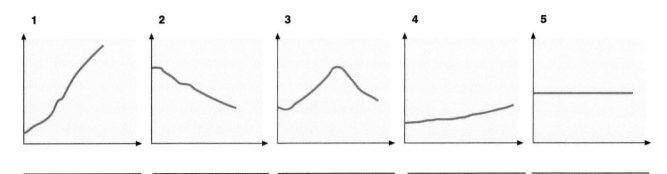

1   2   3   4   5

_____ _____ _____ _____ _____

2 Complete the descriptions of the graphs in *Listening 2* using the phrases in *What do you say? 2*.

Graph 1

The market will _____ at first but then it will develop quickly.

Graph 2

Sales will _____ in the second year but are likely to _____ in the third year.

Graph 3

The price will _____ at first, but will _____ after a year or two.

Note that you can use any of the words and phrases from *Building vocabulary* to describe graphs.

Task 2
Pairs

Objective: Talk about trends

Look at the four graphs below. Choose one and describe it to your partner, using language from *What do you say? 2*. Say simply: 'Sales will ...' Don't say which graph you are describing. Your partner should give the name of the product at the end of your description. Change roles and repeat. Then change partners and practise again.

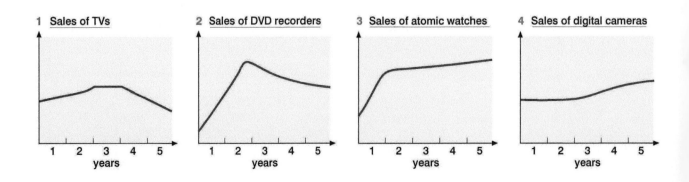

1 Sales of TVs   2 Sales of DVD recorders   3 Sales of atomic watches   4 Sales of digital cameras

1 **Listen to the whole of Lee's presentation again. Number these phrases in the order that he uses them.**

☐ As you can see from the graph ...   ☐ So first, ...

☐ Do you have any questions?   ☐ This graph shows ...

☐ I'd like to talk about ...   ☐ Now let's look at ...

2 **Answer the questions. Listen again and check.**

1   Which phrase does he use to introduce the presentation?

2   Which phrase does he use to introduce the first section?

3   Which phrase does he use to introduce the second section?

4   Which two phrases does he use to talk about the graphs?

5   Which phrase does he use at the end?

Strategies: Giving a short presentation, page 82

Task 3
Whole class in
2 groups

Objective: Present a graph

Step 1   Preparation

You are going to prepare a presentation describing two graphs. Work with two or three people in your group and decide what you want to say.

– Group A turn to page 100.

– Group B turn to page 104.

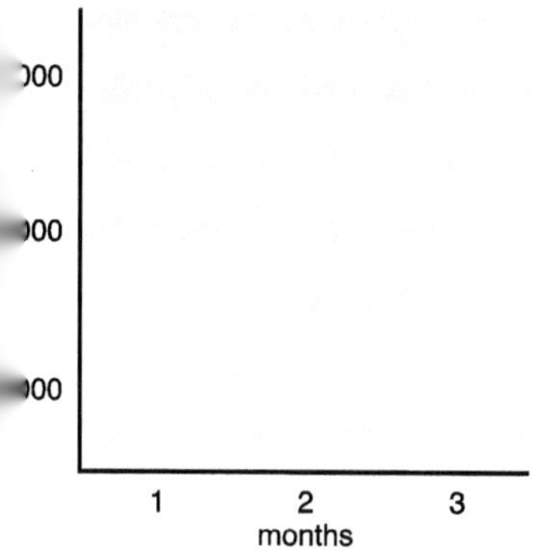

Step 2   Presentation

Pairs

Work with someone from the other group. Give your presentation to your partner, using the language from *Listening 1* and *2*. As you listen to your partner's presentation, complete the blank graphs. Give each graph a title.

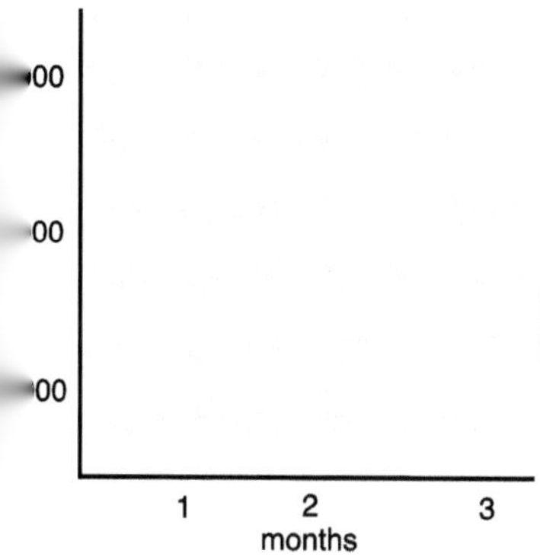

Step 3   Your own presentation

Draw a graph of your own to present to the class. Forecast a future trend, for example, the number of employees in your company, or house prices in your town or country. Follow the instructions.

– Think about the time period that you want to cover (e.g. two years).

– Think about how to describe the graph.

– Decide if your predictions are certain, likely or possible.

Summary

In this unit, you have learnt to:

- make predictions showing if you are certain or uncertain.

- describe graphs and talk about trends

- make a short presentation about a graph

Writing 5 | Messages and notes

| Write a phone message | Write notes on a meeting |

What do you write? 1

Tara Leone is the manager of the north east regional sales office. Her colleague takes a phone message for her. Read the telephone conversation and then complete the written phone message on the left.

Telephone Message

To: Tara Leone
Name of caller:[1]_____
From:[2]_____

Message: Re: the [3]_____ meeting, possible dates are: 14th March, 18th March or 22nd March. Which date is [4]_____? Please call his assistant on 01788125. Also, can you send your [5]_____ for the H111 and the K212 A.SAP

Call taken by: Ingrid
Date: 5th March
Time: 11.30

Ron: Hello, this is Ron Brady from head office. Can I speak to Tara Leone please?

Ingrid: I'm sorry. Tara isn't in the office this morning. Can I take a message?

Ron: Yes, please. I'm calling about the regional sales meeting next month. I'm trying to arrange a date for the meeting. I'd like to give Tara some possible dates. They are: 14th March, 18th March, or 22nd March. I need to know which date is best for Tara.

Ingrid: That's the 14th, 18th or 22nd. OK. I'll ask her to call you this afternoon.

Ron: Oh, I'll probably be in a meeting this afternoon, so perhaps she could call my assistant. Her number is 01788125.

Ingrid: 01788125. OK.

Ron: Also, can she send me her sales forecasts for the H111 and the K212? I need them as soon as possible, please.

Task 1

CD 30

Objective: Write a phone message

Tara calls Ron and speaks to his assistant. Listen to the phone call and write the message which the assistant leaves for Ron.

Telephone Message

To:
Name of caller:
From:

Message:

The marketing department of Condor Electronics held a planning meeting yesterday. Read the marketing manager's summary of the meeting.

Well, the first agenda point was the programme for the visit of the Malaysian team on 23rd June. We discussed the plans for the meeting and we decided that Kim will collect the visitors from their hotel at 8.30 in the morning. We'll need to book the company minibus – Jan, could you do that, please? We decided not to have lunch at the company restaurant but to go to the Orchid Restaurant in town. Jan will book a table for ten at 12.30. Then, in the afternoon, Peter will take the visitors on a tour of the factory.

Next, we discussed the trade conference in Delhi on 29th June. We decided that Fiona and Thomas will go to the conference. Fiona and Thomas, can you check the travel costs for your trip and send the details to the finance office as soon as possible, please?

The third agenda point was staffing problems. We discussed the idea of recruiting more staff and decided that we need two new people. So we're recruiting one person now and the other in six months. John will prepare a job advertisement for the newspapers and Peter will put a notice on the company website.

And finally, we discussed the budget for the next six months. Everyone agreed that costs are going up. We think we'll probably need to increase the budget a little. We want Ricardo to prepare a forecast of spending and we will take a decision at the next planning meeting, which will be on 1st July at 9.00am.

Task 2

Objective: Write notes on a meeting

Look at the summary again and complete these notes on the planning meeting.

Agenda point	Decisions	Action
1 Programme for visit from Malaysian team, 8.30am 23rd June	– Kim will collect visitors from hotel – Lunch at Orchid Restaurant (not company restaurant) –	– Jan to book the company minibus – Jan to book a table for ten at 12.30
2	–	–
3	–	– –
4	–	–

Next meeting: _____

Strategies

Unit 1 — Introducing yourself

Introducing yourself	- Say your first name and family name: - Say your name slowly and clearly:	*Good morning / afternoon.* *I'm John Bates.*
Greeting other people	- New contacts and important people: - People you know well: - It is important to say other people's names correctly. You can ask:	*Good morning / afternoon / evening, Mr Moore.* *Hello, John.* *Sorry, can you say your name again, please?*

Note: In some countries, people use first names from the beginning.

Unit 2 — Introducing other people

General introductions	- Formal: - Informal:	*Can I introduce Mr Jackson?* *This is Gordon.*
People in your team	- Give the job title: - Describe the job:	*He/She is our marketing manager.* *He/She is responsible for sales in the north.*
People from other companies	- Give the company name and job title or department:	*Mr Dawkins works for IBM in the finance department.*

Unit 10 — Meeting people you know

- Greet people you know (informal):	*Good to see you again.*
- Typical first questions:	*How are you? How are things? How's business?*
- Responses to these questions:	*Fine, thanks. I'm very well, thanks. Great! Not too bad, thanks.*
- Say where you last met:	*We last met at the conference in Miami.*
- Ask your friend / colleague what they are doing at the moment:	*What are you doing these days? Are you still ...?*
- Ask about other people you both know:	*How is ...? What is he/she doing?*
- Send greetings to someone you know:	*Please give my regards to Susan. Please give him/her/them my regards.*
- End the conversation:	*It was good to see you again. Good luck with ...*

Unit 3 — Talking about numbers

- Some numbers sound very similar, for example: 13 and 30, 14 and 40, 15 and 50, 16 and 60, 17 and 70, 18 and 80, 19 and 90

  Stress *thirTEEN* or *THIRty* to show the difference. Or say:
  thirteen – that's one-three or *thirty – that's three-zero*
- In English, we write thousands with a comma:

  1,000 (one thousand) 4,250 (four thousand, two hundred and fifty)
- If you don't hear an important number, ask the other person to repeat:

  Sorry, can you repeat that, please?
- Approximate numbers are easier to say:

  98 – about a hundred 968,000 – about a million

Unit 6 — Prices

- When we write, the currency sign goes before the number: $1, €2
- When we speak, the number goes before the currency: *one dollar, two euros*
- There is more than one way to say some prices:

  $2.50: *two dollars, fifty cents / two dollars fifty / two fifty*

  £4.95: *four pounds ninety-five pence / four pounds ninety-five / four ninety-five*
- Other examples:

  £495.00: *four hundred and ninety-five pounds*, €2,000.00: *two thousand euros*,
  $1m: *one million dollars* NOT ~~one million of dollars~~, £5m: *five million pounds*, €10bn: *ten billion euros*
- In emails, we often write the currency code: 50 USD: *50 US dollars*, 25 ZAD:
  25 South African rand

Unit 7 — Dates

- Use ordinal numbers: *1st January, 2nd February, 21st May*
- Use the preposition *on* for days and dates: *on Monday, on 5th May*
- Use the preposition *in* for months and years: *in April, in 2008*

Note the difference between British and US English.

British: 4th June 2008 = 4/6/2008

US: June 4th 2008 = 6/4/2008

Unit 4 Instructions

Giving instructions	Responding to instructions
– *Bring the file!* (not very polite)	*No problem. Certainly.*
– *Can/Could you please bring the file?*	*Yes, of course.*
To give a number of instructions:	To show you understand:
– *Press the button, open the door and go upstairs.*	*Yes. OK. Right.*
(It isn't necessary to say 'Can you please' for each instruction)	

Unit 4 Directions

Asking for directions		Giving directions
– *Excuse me.*		
– *How do I get to ...?*		*Go straight on.*
– *Can you please tell me the way to ...?*	River Street	*Go along River Street.*
		Take the first turning right.
		Take the second turning left.
		Cross the street.
	Station Hotel	*Go past the Station Hotel.*
	Restaurant	*The restaurant is on your right.*
	Station	*It's in front of the station.*
		It's on the corner.
	Station	*It's near the station.*
	cafe hotel	*It's between the hotel and the café.*

Repeating to check	Confirming
– *Go along River Street.*	*That's right.*
– *On the left?*	*Yes.*

Thanking	Confirming
– *Thank you for your help.*	*No problem.*
	You're welcome.

Unit 5 | Requests

Requesting politely	Responding to requests
– Can/Could I have rice, please?	Certainly.
– I'd like water, please. [= I would like]	Of course.
– Could I have the menu / Could you bring the menu, please ...?	No problem.
– Please can you bring the menu?	I'm sorry, I can't.
	I'm sorry, we don't have that.

Unit 5 | Offers and opinions

Offering politely	Responding to offers
– Would you like roast potatoes?	Yes, please. That would be very nice.
– What would you like to drink / to start with?	No potatoes, thank you. Just a salad.
	I'd like water, please.

Giving an opinion	Responding to an opinion
– I like steak!	I like it, too. I don't like it.
– It's excellent / delicious / very good.	Yes, it is!

Asking about opinions	Responding
– Do you like fish?	Yes, it's delicious. It's very good.
	I'm sorry, but I don't like chicken very much.

Unit 8 | Asking for help and being helpful

Asking for help	Being helpful
– Can you help me, please?	Can I help (you)? How can I help?
– I have a problem with ...	Oh, dear. I'm sorry about that.
– I think there's something wrong with ...	Don't worry. I'm sure we can fix it.
Explain what happened. Describe what you did or didn't do:	What's the problem?
	What did you do? Did you ...?
	Let me have a look.
	I'll ask someone to come and have a look at it.

Unit 9 — Talking about products

- Introduce the product:

  I'd like to tell you about the Digital Photo Album.

- Say what the product does or what you use it for:

  It stores up to 2,000 digital photos.

  You use it for storing and showing your digital photos.

- Say why it is special:

  You don't need a PC to show your photos. It's very easy to use.

- Use strong, positive adjectives:

  It's new, it's exciting and it's practical.

- Give information about size and weight:

  It is 18 centimetres long and 7 centimetres wide.

  It weighs 85 grams.

- Say what it is made of:

  It's made of metal.

- Say that it isn't expensive:

  It costs only 25 dollars.

Unit 11 — Discussing ideas

- Give a positive opinion:

  I think it's very nice.

  In my opinion it's very nice.

- Give a negative opinion:

  I don't think it's very nice.

  It isn't big enough.

  It's too big.

- Agree with other people:

  I agree.

  That's right.

  You're right.

- In some countries, it is not polite to disagree. It is better to say you are not sure.
  Or you can say something positive and then say 'but ...' and give your own opinion:

  I'm not sure about that.

  Yes, we need a big place, but not too big.

  Perhaps you are right, but I think it is too big.

- Ask someone for their opinion:

  What do you think?

  What's your opinion?

- In a group, check if everyone is happy with a decision:

  Does everyone agree?

Asking questions

- Use open questions to ask for specific information:

    Question words: *when, where, what, who, how, why, how much, how many, how long, how far*

    Where did you study?

    When did you start your present job?

    Why do you want a new job?

    What are your main interests?

    Who do you work for?

    How did you hear about this job?

    How long have you worked in finance?

- If you want a simple yes or no answer, ask closed questions:

    Do you like travelling?

    Did you enjoy your trip?

    Have you ever been to the US?

    Are you still working for IBM?

- Sometimes, it is useful to ask a very open question to get general information. This is a useful strategy at the start of a meeting or interview. (Note that we don't usually ask these questions in social situations.):

    Can you tell me a bit about yourself?

    What can you tell me about your present job?

- If the other person didn't give you enough information, you can ask:

    Can you tell me a bit more about that?

Meetings

Leading a meeting

- Start the meeting:

    Welcome to the meeting.

- Explain the problem or the purpose of the meeting:

    As you know, we are here to discuss ...

    The problem is ...

    We need to decide ...

    Should we ...?

- Ask people for opinions or ideas:

    What do people think?

    Sam, what do you think?

    Any other ideas?

- Ask someone to do something:

    Justine, would you like to ...

Taking part in a meeting

- Ask for a chance to speak:

    Can I please say something?

    I'd like to ask a question.

- Ask when you don't understand something:

    Sorry, I didn't follow that. Can you please say it again, slowly?

- Make a suggestion and give the reason:

    I think we should ... because ...

Unit 14 | Telephoning

Answering the phone

- Say your name and the name of your department or company:

    Hello. / Good morning. Sales office. Paul speaking.

- When the caller asks for someone who isn't there:

    I'm afraid Mr Potts isn't in the office at the moment.

- Offer to take a message:

    Can I take a message?

    Can I ask him to call you back? Can you give me your number?

- To promise action, use *I'll* ... (= *I will* ...):

    I'll give him your message.

    I'll ask him to call you back.

- Note: when you take a call for someone else, be sure to get the caller's name, company and telephone number. Check the details carefully and ask for repetition if you need to.

Making a call

- Introduce yourself:

    Hello. This is Jane Kelly from Greenshanks. (NOT ~~I am Jane Kelly~~ ...)

    My name is Jane Kelly.

- Check if you have the right person or department:

    Is that David Potts? (NOT ~~Are you David Potts?~~)

- Explain what the call is about:

    I'm calling about our meeting next week.

    I'd like to arrange a meeting.

Unit 15 | Giving a short presentation

- At the start, say what you will talk about:

    I'd like to talk about ...

- If you have different points to make, say that you will divide your talk into sections:

    First, I'll talk about ...

    Then I'll tell you ...

    And finally, I'll present ...

- Introduce each section:

    So first, ...

    Now let's look at ...

    Now I'd like to present ...

- At the end, give a short summary:

    So that was ...

    So, to sum up ...

- Give the audience time to ask questions:

    Do you have any questions?

Grammar reference

to be

Form

- *to be* has the forms *am ('m), is ('s) and are ('re)* in the present

  I'm a teacher.

  He's from Tokyo.

  They're at a conference.

- the contracted form is used mainly in spoken English and the full form in formal writing

  Hi, I'm Paul.

  My name is Paul Edwards. I am an engineer.

  These three countries are all in Europe.

- the word *not* is added to make negatives; we contract *is not* and *are not* to *isn't* and *aren't*

  I'm not sure.

  He isn't French.

  They aren't engineers.

- the verb goes before the subject in questions, and the contractions *'m, 's, 're* are not used.

  Is he Belgian?

  Are they from Tokyo?

- the contracted form is not used in affirmative short answers

  Are you from Spain? Yes, I am.

  Is she the head of the company?

  Yes, she is.

  Is he the head of the company?

  No, he isn't.

Exercises

1 Complete the sentences with the correct form of the verb to *be*.

A: Hello. I ¹_____ Atsuko Kondo, from Japan. And this ²____ my colleague, Jolanta Migon. We ³_____ both engineers.

B: Can I introduce Fernando Lopez and Raul Suarez. Fernando and Raul ⁴____ both lawyers. They ⁵_____ with Banco de Santander. It ⁶____ a very big bank in Spain.

2 Write questions. Use the words in brackets and the correct form of the verb *to be*.

1 What country ___ ___ from? (you)
2 ___ ___ both American? (they)
3 ____ ____ ready to start? (we)
4 What ___ ___ ___? (your name)
5 ____ ____ French? (Monique)
6 What ___ ___ job? (Peter's)

3 Make these sentences negative.

1 I'm a finance manager.
2 Yvette is British.
3 Barbara and Marina are with Siemens.
4 Shell is an American company.
5 That's Fiona McDonald.
6 We are personnel managers.

Present simple affirmative

Form

- the form of the present simple affirmative does not change except for adding *s* in the third person
  I/You/We/They **work** *for a big company.*
  He/She/It **works** ...

Note: the third person singular of *have* is *has*; *do* and *go* change to *does* and *goes* in the third person singular

The present simple has the following uses.

- routines or regular activities
  We **have** *lunch at this restaurant.*
  They usually **meet** *twice a month.*
  She always **arrives** *early at the office.*
  I **catch** *the 8.15 train every day.*
- permanent or long-term situations
  They **work** *for an international company.*
  She **has** *a good job in IT.*

Key words

these words go between the subject and the main verb (but after *to be*): *always, usually, often, sometimes, never*
these words usually go at the end of the sentence: *every day / week / month / year*

Present simple negative, question and short answer

Form

- negative: I / You / We / They **don't work.**
                     He / She / It **doesn't work.**

- question: **Do** I / you / we / they **work?**
                     Does he / she / it **work?**

- short answer: Yes, **I do.** Yes, she **does.**
                        No, they **don't.** No, he **doesn't.**

- the auxiliary verb *do/does* is used for negative sentences, questions and short answers
  Jenny **doesn't** *drive.*
  Do *they work for IBM? Yes, they* **do.**
  Does *she live there? No, she* **doesn't.**
  Where **does** *she live?*

Exercises

1 Complete the text with the correct form of the verbs in brackets.

Michael O'Hara [1](live) _____ in Dublin and [2](manage) _____ a taxi company. Michael [3](have) _____ 16 drivers in his company. The drivers often [4](meet) _____ foreign visitors from the airport. Bridget and Dervla [5](work) _____ as secretaries in Michael's company. They [6](answer) _____ the telephone and [7](take) _____ messages for the drivers. Michael [8](organise) _____ all the work.

2 Put the words in brackets into the sentences.

1 (usually) I start work at 8 am
2 (never) I'm late for work.
3 (always) Kate is at the office first.
4 (often) Paula travels on business.
5 (every day) We have a lot of visitors.

Exercises

1 Complete the sentences with the correct form of *do*.

1 _____ you live in Hong Kong?
2 Yes, I _____.
3 _____ your company have subsidiaries?
4 No, it _____.
5 _____ they make paper?
6 No, they _____ – they make packaging.
7 _____ John and Lisa work in Paris?
8 Well, yes, John _____, but Lisa _____ – she works in Bonn.

Articles

- the **indefinite article** is used to talk about things in general
  Do you have a mobile phone?
  He works in an office.
- *a* is used before a singular noun beginning with a consonant sound
  a document, a salesperson, a university
- *an* is used before a singular noun beginning with a vowel sound
  an accountant, an office, an umbrella
- the plural of *a/an* can be *some*, *any* or no article (zero article) (see **Countable and uncountable nouns**, page 88)
- the **definite article** is used to talk about specific things
  Do you have the new Nokia phone?
  He works in the office next to the station.
- *the* is used for both the singular and the plural
- *the* is pronounced ði: before a word that begins with a vowel sound and ðə before a word that begins with a consonant sound

The imperative

Form

- affirmative: infinitive of the verb without *to*
  Plug in your laptop.
- negative: *don't* + infinitive without *to*
  Don't open the window.

The imperative has the following uses.

- instructions
  Turn left at reception.
  Attach the mouse to the computer.
- orders
  Tidy your desk.
  Don't go into the manager's office, please.

Note: to ask, instead of order, someone to do something, we use *can*

Can you tidy your desk, please?

or *could* to be more polite

Could you tidy your desk, please?

Exercises

1 Complete the sentences with *a/an* or *the*.

1 I work for _____ insurance company.
2 It's _____ Belgian company.
3 Mrs Fortyn is _____ CEO.
4 This is _____ company's head office.
5 We also have _____ office in Antwerp.
6 I'm _____ lawyer and I work in _____ legal department.
7 This is Mr Goosens. He is _____ Head of Department.
8 I'm on _____ trip round _____ world.

Exercises

1 Which is correct, a or b?

1 a Please open the window.
   b Please to open the window
2 a Put you the file on the desk.
   b Put the file on the desk.
3 a Please don't smoke in the office.
   b Please don't to smoke in the office.
4 a Wait for me on the corner.
   b You to wait on the corner.
5 a Don't you put food in the bin.
   b Don't put food in the bin.

2 Complete the instructions for finding someone's office with these words.

Go Don't Look Open press turn Type
Next to the main door, there is a security system.
¹ _____ the number 4109 and ² _____ OK. ³ _____ the door. ⁴ _____ use the lift – it doesn't work.
⁵ _____ up the stairs. At the top of the stairs, ⁶ _____ right. ⁷ _____ for room 102.

Prepositions of place

■ we use these prepositions to describe **where** things are

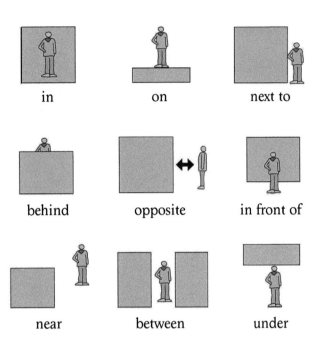

in   on   next to

behind   opposite   in front of

near   between   under

*He lives **near** the station.*

*There are two computers **in** my office.*

there is and there are

■ we often use *there is* or *there are* when we describe **what** is in a place

Singular	Plural
There is (There's) a file next to the PC.	There are six pens on the desk.
There is not (There isn't) a file next to the PC.	There are not (There aren't) six pens on the desk.

Exercises

1 **Look at the picture. Complete the sentences with these words and phrases.**

between   in front of   in
opposite   on   under

1   I usually keep pens _____ the top drawer of the desk.
2   My in-tray is _____ the desk.
3   The phone is _____ the PC and the in-tray.
4   My shoes are _____ the desk.
5   The desk is _____ a window.
6   The chair is _____ the desk.

2 **Complete these sentences about the picture with *there is / isn't / aren't* or *is there / are there*.**

1   _____ a PC on the desk?
2   Yes, _____.
3   _____ six drawers?
4   No, _____. There are five.
5   _____ a printer on the desk?
6   No, _____. There's a telephone.

Modal verbs *can* and *would*

Form

- most modal verbs are followed by the infinitive without *to*
  I **can help** you.
- *would like* is followed by the infinitive with *to*
  I**'d like to have** lunch at 1.00.
- modal verbs do not use *do* in questions or *don't* in the negative
  Can she use a computer?
  We **can't** come on Tuesday.
- modal verbs do not take *s* in the third person singular
  Good food **can** be expensive.

Can has the following uses.

- ability
  I **can** cook.
  They **can't** speak German.
- possibility
  We **can** meet at the restaurant.
  They **can't** come next week.
- requests
  Can you help me, please?
  or *could* to be more polite
  Could I have the bill, please?

Would is used for polite offers and requests.

Would you like coffee?
I**'d** (= I **would**) like to reserve a table for tonight.

Note:
I**'d like** coffee. (request)
I **like** coffee. (general comment)

Exercises

1 Mark the sentences P (possibility) or A (ability).

1 David can speak Japanese. ☐
2 It can be very hot in summer. ☐
3 This car can do 200 kilometres per hour. ☐
4 I'm sorry – I can't cook. ☐
5 I can't see you tomorrow – I'm busy. ☐

2 Write questions or requests. Use *can* and the prompts.

1 we / have / the bill?
2 you / please / bring / the menu?
3 Anna / play / the guitar?
4 Where / I / buy / bus tickets?
5 the engineers / design / a new model?
6 When / they / start / work?

3 Write offers or requests. Use *would* or *'d* and the prompts.

1 we / like / a table for four / please
2 you / like / to sit by the window?
3 you / like / a drink to start with?
4 we / like / some water / please
5 I / like / the bill / please
6 how / you / like / to pay?

Countable and uncountable nouns

Countable nouns have a singular and plural form.

- we use *a/an* with singular countable nouns
  *I'd like to buy **a** new car.*
- we use *some* with plural countable nouns in affirmative sentences
  *We need **some** pictures for the office.*

Uncountable nouns do not have a plural form.
sugar, information, time, money

Note: *money* is uncountable, but notes, coins, dollars, etc. are countable.

- we use *some* with uncountable nouns in affirmative sentences
  *I'd like **some** information about prices.*

---

some, any, how much/many

- we use *some* in affirmative sentences but we use *any* in negative sentences and real questions; we use *any* with both countable and uncountable nouns
  *There aren't **any** glasses.*
  *Do you have **any** red pens?*
  *Is there **any** water in the bottle?*
  *We don't have **any** money in the bank.*

Note: we use *some* for requests and offers
*Could I have **some** water?*

- we use *how many* with countable nouns for questions about quantity
  *How **many** managers are there?*
- we use *how much* with uncountable nouns for questions about quantity or price
  *How **much** time do we have?*
  *How **much** is the coffee?*

Exercises

1 **Complete the sentences with *a/an* or *some.***

1 We have _____ special offer: two for the price of one.
2 Can I order _____ caviar, please?
3 We need _____ money to pay the taxi.
4 Would you like _____ envelope for your notes?

2 **Complete the conversation with *a, some* or *any.***

A: Excuse me. Do you have ¹_____ coloured paper?
B: What colours would you like?
A: I'd like blue, green and yellow. ²_____ pack of each, please.
B: We have ³_____ yellow and green paper in stock, but we don't have ⁴_____ blue at the moment. I can order ⁵_____ for you.
A: OK. Can I order ⁶_____ pack of 500 sheets of blue then, please?

---

3 **Complete the conversation with *much* or *many.***

A: Excuse me. How ¹_____ are the oranges, please?
B: They're 50 cents each. How ²_____ would you like?
A: Just four, please.
B: They're only 40 cents if you buy more.
A: How ³_____ do I need to buy?
B: Eight.
A: And how ⁴_____ do I pay then?
B: €3.20. Is that OK?
A: Yes, that's fine, thanks.
B: Anything else?
A: How ⁵_____ is the olive oil?
B: It's €2 for half a litre, or €3.50 for a litre.
A: I'd like a litre, please.

Past simple affirmative

Form

- the past simple is formed by adding -ed to the infinitive of regular verbs
  started, finished
- regular verbs ending in *e* just add -d
  arrived, decided
- there are many irregular verbs
  be – was/were, do – did, have – had, take – took

Note: most dictionaries have a list of irregular verbs

- the form of the past simple does not change
  *I/You/He/She/(It)/We/They **worked** late.*
  except to *be*
  *I/He/She/(It) **was** at home.*
  *You/We/They **were** at the office.*

The past simple has the following uses.

- events that happened at a definite time in the past
  *They **arrived** last Tuesday.*
  *The meeting **was** last week.*
- finished actions and events
  *The project **started** in May and **finished** last month.*

Time expressions

We often use the past simple tense with these expressions.

at + clock time

on + day, date

in + *the morning/afternoon/evening, month / season / year*

yesterday, last week/month/year, ago

*We started **at 9.15 on Monday**.*

*I went to Brazil **in August**.*

*They met **two years ago**.*

Exercises

1 **Complete the text with the past simple of the verbs in brackets.**

In 1997, Sue ¹(visit) _____ a market. There ²(be) _____ some paintings for sale. She ³(buy) _____ a painting, and it ⁴(cost) _____ €20. Last year, she ⁵(show) _____ the painting to an art dealer. The dealer ⁶(offer) _____ her €10,000 for the painting. Sue ⁷(sell) _____ the painting to him and ⁸(make) _____ a very good profit.

2 **Complete the sentences with *in*, *on* or *at*.**

1 The meeting started _____ 9am.
2 We first met _____ 2007.
3 We went home at ten ___ the evening.
4 We agreed to meet _____ 1st July.
5 The conference was ___ October.
6 I visited Warsaw ___ summer.

3 **Complete the sentences with *ago* or *last*.**

1 We made the decision two years _____.
2 _____ year, the building work began.
3 We finished building six months _____.
4 _____ month, we installed machines.
5 We tested the machines _____ week.
6 Two days _____, we produced our first pair of shoes.

Past simple negative, question and short answer

Negative	Question
I didn't work.	Did I work?
You didn't work.	Did you work?
She didn't work.	Did she work?
We didn't work.	Did we work?
They didn't work.	Did they work?

Short answer
Yes, I/you/he/she/it we/they did.
No, I/you/he/she/it we/they didn't.

- The auxiliary verb *did* (the past tense of *do*) is used for negative sentences, questions and short answers

  I **didn't** see you at the meeting yesterday.

  Did you enjoy the meal?

  What **did** you have to eat?

  Did you go to the conference?

  Yes, I **did**.

  Did Glyn go?

  No, he **didn't**.

Exercises

1 **Write open questions. Use the words in brackets.**

I called the engineer. (Who) *Who did you call?*

1   I went to Scotland last week. (When)
2   I stayed at the Tartan Hotel. (Where)
3   I met some colleagues from our Scottish office. (Who)
4   The meeting was about technical problems. (What)

2 **Write closed questions.**

We enjoyed the food.

Did you enjoy the food?

1   There was a golf course at the hotel.
2   We played golf.
3   We had a good time.
4   The company paid for everything.

3 **Make these sentences negative.**

1   There were many people at the meeting.
2   The projector worked.
3   I showed my pictures.
4   People asked questions.
5   They were very interested.
6   My presentation was a success.

Key to exercise 3
1 There weren't many people at the meeting.
2 The projector didn't work. 3 I didn't show my pictures. 4 People didn't ask questions. 5 They weren't very interested. 6 My presentation wasn't a success.

Key to exercise 2
1 Was there a golf course at the hotel? 2 Did you play golf? 3 Did you have a good time? 4 Did the company pay for everything?

Key to exercise 1
1 When did you go to Scotland? 2 Where did you stay? 3 Who did you meet? 4 What was the meeting about?

Adjectives and adverbs

Adjectives

- describe a noun

  a **new** product

  some **good** friends

  the **early** train

- do not change if the noun is plural

  a **new** market

  some **new** markets

- go before the noun

  a **light** laptop

- go after the verb *to be* and certain other verbs, e.g. *look, feel, sound*

  The laptop **is small**.

  It **looks** very **light**.

Adverbs

- give information about a verb

  He talks **slowly**.

  They listened **carefully**.

  She works very **hard**.

- are usually formed by adding *-ly* to an adjective

  quick – quickly

- adjectives ending in *-y* drop the *y* and add *-ily* to form the adverb

  easy – easily

- adjectives ending in *-ic* add *-ally* to form the adverb

  automatic – automatically

- some adverbs are irregular

  good – well, fast – fast, hard – hard

Exercises

1 Put the words into the correct order.

1 20cm / The / toy / high / is .
2 Is / reliable / camera / this / a ?
3 stylish / shoes / are / They .
4 comfortable / feel / They / very .
5 car / It's / very / a / economical .
6 book / This / interesting / looks .

2 Change the adjectives to adverbs and complete the sentences.

1 You can (easy) _____ download your photos to a PC.
2 Children can play (safe) _____ with this equipment.
3 Learn English (fast) _____ with this new CD.
4 You need to read the instructions (careful) _____ .
5 I speak English (good) _____ .
6 The cooker turns off (automatic) _____ when the food is ready.

3 Complete the sentences. Choose the correct words in *italics*.

1 I'm not *happy / happily* with this printer.
2 It doesn't print *good / well*.
3 The camera has a *large / largely* screen.
4 It's made of very *strong / strongly* steel.
5 It cooks food *perfect / perfectly*.
6 Tell me about your trip – it sounds *interesting / interestingly*.

Present continuous

Form

- the present continuous is formed by using *am / is / are* (see **to be**, page 83) and adding *-ing* to the infinitive of the verb

Affirmative	Negative
I'm working.	I'm not working.
You're working.	You aren't working.
He/She/It is working.	He/She/It isn't working.
We're working.	We aren't working.
They're working.	They aren't working.

Questions
Am I working?
Are you/we/they working?
Is he/she/it working?

I'm waiting for my colleague.
Are you increasing your exports?
He isn't working in China now.

The present continuous has the following uses.

- things that are happening now
  I'm speaking on the phone.
- temporary actions and situations
  We're having problems in the European market this year.

Note: We use the **Present simple** (see page 84) for routines or regular activities, and for permanent or long-term situations.

Key words

at the moment, currently, now, just/right now, this week/month/year

Exercises

1 **Mark the sentences N (happening now), T (temporary) or R (regular/routine).**

1 I'm having lunch – can we talk later?
2 The boss is on holiday – I'm managing the team this week.
3 We usually leave early on Friday.
4 I'm learning to use the new machine.
5 They're painting my office this week, so I'm working in a different place.
6 Our suppliers normally deliver on Monday.

2 **Complete the sentences with the present continuous of the verbs in brackets.**

1 I (prepare) _____ the report right now.
2 Miss West (wait) _____ for you at Reception.
3 Jenny and Paul (discuss) _____ the new plan.
4 Leila (not answer) _____ her phone – I think she's in a meeting.
5 We (not take) _____ orders at present – the computer's down.
6 I (not enjoy) _____ my job at the moment.
7 (Roger, still work) _____ in your office?
8 What (you, draw) _____?

3 **Complete the conversation with the present continuous or present simple of the verbs in brackets.**

A: We usually ¹(get) _____ coffee from the machine, but it ²(not work) _____ at the moment.

B: Those machines ³(not make) _____ good coffee, so I'm not sorry.

A: The restaurant ⁴(serve) _____ lunch right now so we can't have coffee there.

B: There's a café on the corner that ⁵(sell) _____ coffee. They ⁶(offer) _____ a special deal this week: a free cake with every coffee!

A: OK, let's go!

Comparatives and superlatives

Comparatives

Form

	Adjective	Comparative
1 or 2 syllables	big	bigger
2 syllables ending in -y	happy	happier
2+ syllables	important	more important

- the **comparative** is used to compare two things. We don't always name both.

  *London is often **warmer than** Madrid.*

  *Moscow is **more expensive than** Paris.*

  *The 8pm train is **quicker**.*

- some comparatives are irregular

  good – better, bad – worse,
  far – further/farther

Superlatives

Form

	Adjective	Superlative
1 or 2 syllables	big	the biggest
2 syllables ending in -y	happy	the happiest
2+ syllables	important	the most important

- the **superlative** is used to compare one person or thing in a group with the whole group

  *Winter is **the coldest** time of year.*

  *He stays in **the most expensive** hotels.*

- some superlatives are irregular

  good – best, bad – worst, far – furthest/farthest

too and enough

- we use *too* before an adjective when it is more than we want or need

  *It is **too hot** to work in August.*

  *That hotel is **too expensive** (for us)*

- we use *not enough* when we want or need more of something

  *There **isn't enough** space for three cars.*

  *The room **isn't** big **enough** for 30 people.*

Exercises

1 Complete the sentences with the comparative form of the adjectives in brackets.

1 My old office was (quiet) _____ than this.
2 The Box café is (cheap) _____ than the Ace restaurant.
3 Hans is a (good) _____ presenter than me.
4 The test results were (bad) _____ than last year.
5 The tests are (difficult) _____ than before.
6 The new model is (practical) _____ than the older models.

2 Complete the sentences with the superlative form of the adjectives in brackets.

1 Sue's home is the (near) _____ to the office.
2 Jacqui has the (beautiful) _____ house.
3 Fred's house is the (far) _____ from town.
4 Sue has the (interesting) _____ job.
5 Fred drives the (large) _____ car.

3 Correct the mistakes.

1 Steel is stronger to plastic.
2 Sam is the worse driver in the team.
3 Your report isn't enough good.
4 The new car is to big for my garage.
5 Japan has fastest trains in the world.
6 This exercise is more easy than the last one.

Present perfect

Form

- the present perfect is formed by using *have* or *has* and the past participle of the verb

Affirmative	Negative
I/You/We/They have paid.	I/You/We/They have not paid.
He/She/It has paid.	He/She/It has not paid.

Question
Have I/you/we/they paid?
Has he/she/it paid?

- in the affirmative, we contract *have* and *has* to *'ve* and *'s*
  They've lived in a lot of different countries.
- in the negative, we use *haven't* and *hasn't*
  He hasn't been to China.

The present perfect has the following use.

- talking about experience (often with *ever / never*)
  We've been to Venice.
  He's never had an interview before.
  Have you ever visited the pyramids?
  No, I haven't.

---

for and *since*

The present perfect also has the following use.

- activities that started in the past and continue to the present (answering the question *How long ...?*)
  How long have you worked at J&C?
  I've worked in this job for six months.
  (I'm still in this job.)
  I've been with the company since 2006.
  (I'm still with the company.)
- *for* + number of days / months / years
  I've worked here for a year.
- *since* + a time in the past
  He has worked here since July 2007.

Note: we can also use *for* with the past simple for finished time periods
I worked in London for six years.
(I don't work there now.)

Exercises

1 **Complete the sentences with the present perfect of the verbs in brackets.**

1 They (study) _____ English for three years.
2 Rob (not, meet) _____ his new boss.
3 I (work) _____ in this department since 1999.
4 (you, apply) _____ for any other jobs?
5 Louis (never, drive) _____ a sports car.

---

2 **Complete the sentences with *for*, *since*, *ever* or *never*.**

1 I've lived in the same house _____ 20 years.
2 My African colleagues have _____ seen snow.
3 We've been married _____ 1996.
4 Have you _____ worked in IT?
5 The meeting lasted _____ six hours.
6 He hasn't called _____ yesterday.

3 **Is the action finished or not?**

1 I stayed with the company for six months.
2 He's been my manager for a year.
3 Lisa has lived in Los Angeles for two years.
4 We had no work for three months.

Modal verbs *could* and *should*

Form

See **Modal verbs *can* and *would*,** page 87.

***Could* has the following uses.**

- polite requests
  ***Could** I have the bill, please?*
- suggestions
  *I **could** drive you to the airport.*
  *He **could** speak to the IT department.*

Note: could is also the past of can

*We **couldn't** go to the conference yesterday, but we can go today.*

***Should* has the following use.**

- to give advice
  *You **should** design a new logo.*
  *You **shouldn't** do business with them.*

Infinitive +/- *to*

- most modal verbs are followed by the infinitive without *to* (see page 87)
- some verbs are followed by the infinitive with *to*
  *They **want to go** to the circus.*
  *Do we **need to take** a taxi?*

> **Key words**
> *agree, ask, decide, forget, need, offer, plan, promise, refuse, want*

Exercises

1 **Complete the sentences with *could* or *should*.**

1 You _____ look for a new supplier. (advice)
2 You _____ try Kelly & Co – they're good! (suggestion)
3 You _____n't tell anyone about this. (advice)
4 They _____ wait for a better offer. (advice)
5 He _____n't send the documents by email. (advice)
6 We _____ break for lunch now. (suggestion)

2 **Complete the sentences with *could*, *should*, *couldn't* or *shouldn't*.**

1 _____ you help me to carry this box, please?
2 You _____ smoke at the petrol station – it's dangerous.
3 Six months ago, I _____ speak any English, but now I know a lot!
4 I think you _____ leave early because ...
5 ... there _____ be a lot of traffic later.

---

3 **Which sentences need *to*?**

1 We plan _____ hold the meeting at ten.
2 You should _____ keep your money safe.
3 I didn't agree _____ write the report.
4 They promised _____ send it today.
5 You could _____ make a new offer.
6 I've decided _____ take a holiday.

Key to exercise 3
sentences 1, 3, 4 and 6 need *to*

Key to exercise 2
1 Could 2 shouldn't 3 couldn't 4 should 5 could

Key to exercise 1
1 should 2 could 3 should 4 should 5 should 6 could

Present continuous for future

We usually use the present continuous to talk about things that are happening now and for temporary actions and situations (see **Present continuous**, page 92).

The present continuous also has the following use.

- things that are arranged for a fixed time in the future

  I'm travelling to Prague next week.

  Is the plane **leaving** at 2pm on Monday?

---

will for decisions and predictions

Form

will + infinitive without to

- affirmative: *I will (I'll) / He will (He'll) / They will (They'll) call.*

- negative: *will not* (usually as contraction: *won't*) *I won't call. They won't call.*

- question: *Will you/she/they call?*

will has the following uses.

- making decisions at the time of speaking

  A: I heard there's a lot of traffic today.

  B: That's OK – **I'll take** the train.

- making predictions about the future

  We **will get** the contract.

  House prices **won't increase** in the next five years.

Exercises

1 Mark the sentences P (present) or F (future).

1 I'm going to the theatre tonight.
2 What are you doing on Wednesday?
3 We're interviewing candidates next week.
4 Bob's talking on the phone right now.
5 The visitors are leaving tomorrow.

2 Complete the arrangements using the present continuous of the verbs in brackets.

1 We (meet) _____ at the airport at 7am.
2 Carla (not, bring) _____ the samples.
3 The plane (arrive) _____ in Madrid at 11.
4 David and Filipo (drive) _____.
5 (we stay) _____ at the Coruna Hotel?

Key to exercise 2
1 We're meeting 2 is not bringing 3 is arriving
4 are driving 5 Are we staying

Key to exercise 1
1 F 2 F 3 F 4 P 5 F

Exercises

1 Decisions. Write responses with 'll and the verb in brackets.

1 A: What would you like?
   B: I (have) the soup, please.
2 A: Who will start the discussion?
   B: I (start).
3 A: Sorry, Mr Jones isn't here.
   B: That's OK. I (call) later.

2 Predictions. Write sentences with 'll or won't using the verbs in brackets.

1 Of course he (finish) on schedule.
2 Don't worry, it (not, be) a problem.
3 I'm certain they (accept) our offer.
4 We (not find) a cheaper deal.

Key to exercise 2
1 he'll finish 2 it won't be 3 they'll accept 4 We won't find

Key to exercise 1
1 I'll have the soup, please. 2 I'll start. 3 I'll call later.

Pairwork

Unit 1   Task 2   Page 8

Student A

Name	Wendy Goolagong
Company	Joshua Zarbutt & Co
Job	Architect
Nationality	Australian

Unit 1   Task 3   Page 9

Student A

Visitor information

Name: Michael Knight
Company: TY Motors Ltd
To see: Mr Lennox (finance manager)

Unit 2   Task 2   Page 12

Group A

Marketing manager
Responsibility: promotion of the company's products

Activities: lead the marketing team; discuss marketing ideas; co-ordinate marketing activities

Unit 3   Task 3   Page 17

Student A

Company: Choix – a retail company
Sells: clothing
Headquarters: Paris, France
Subsidiaries: 17
Number of stores: 730 (400 in France, 330 in other countries in Europe)
Employees: 4,500
Sales: 2 billion euros
CEO: Solange Poiret

Unit 4   Task 2   Page 22

Student A

1 You need your diary. Location: desk – top drawer.
2 You need a new notebook. Location: cupboard – middle shelf.
3 You need the Company Report. Location: small table – under books.

Unit 6   Task 1   Page 29

Student A

Supplier
(100 cents = one dollar / $1)
Apples – $1 / kilo
Beef – $14 / kilo
Mineral water – $0.50 / litre
Tomatoes – $0.47 / tin (500 grams)
Potatoes – $0.25 / kilo
Milk – $0.60 / litre

Unit 6   Task 2   Page 30

Student A

Supplier
This is what you have/don't have in stock:
- G500 Photo Printer – you have 1 in stock. Price $135
- Printer cartridges, multi-colour – you have lots in stock.
- Photo paper: You have lots in stock.
- Bluetooth adapter – you have 10 in stock.
- Folders (for photos) – out of stock.

Unit 6   Task 3   Page 31

Student A

Buyer
Customer details
Name: Chris Revallo
Company name: KG Autos
Customer account number: 979601

Unit 6 Task 3 Page 31

Student A

Supplier: Price list

Envelopes
EVWA4 (White A4, pack of 500): $9.90
EVWA5 (White A5, pack of 500): $7.85
EVBA4 (Brown A4, pack of 500): $6.60

Paper for photocopier
CP804 (White A4, pack of 500 sheets): $10.25
CP803 (White A3, pack of 500 sheets): $21. 99

Printer cartridges
GE490 (Black): $9.30 each
JA685 (Multi-colour): $49.60 each

Desk diaries
DDQ07 (Executive desk diary): $17.25 each
DDK07 (Standard desk diary): $10.50 each

Unit 7 Task 3 Page 37

Student A
Today is 9th December

Project: To install a new machine in the factory

Make a decision to buy a new machine:
1st August

Look at different machines and choose the best one: August

Negotiate with the suppliers:
August–September

Place an order for the machine: end of September

Suppliers deliver the machine: 30th October

They install the machine: beginning of November

They test it: November

We start production with the new machine:
8th December

Unit 8 Task 3 Page 41

Student A

Correct procedure for problem 2
1 Turn your camera on.
2 Use the USB cable.
3 Connect the camera to the computer's USB port.
4 Click on the photo wizard.
5 Follow the steps in the photo wizard.

(**Solution:** B didn't turn on the camera first.)

Unit 9 Task 2 Page 45

Student A

Product 1 Orange peeler
For peeling oranges
Made of metal and plastic
Size: length = 60mm, width = 35mm
Why special: easy to use, can carry it in your pocket
Price: €5.80

Product 3 Bike in a bag
Carry it on the train, ride it in the city
Made of strong steel
Size (in the bag): length = 72 cm, width = 30cm, height = 57cm, weight = 11.8kg
Why special: easy to pack, easy to carry
Price: €299

Unit 9 Task 1 Page 43

Student A

Adult's sports tricycle
Height = 67 cm   Length = 180 cm
Width = 78 cm   Weight = 19.5 kg

Unit 2 Task 2 Page 12

Group A

Export sales assistant
Responsibility: sales to other countries
Activities: travel to different countries; meet customers; take orders by phone and email

Unit 11 Task 3 Page 55

Student A

Centre A: Durban

Accommodation	Rooms for 2,000 people
Exhibition space	5,000 square metres
From the airport	40 km (1 hour by road)
Special feature	Excellent leisure facilities
Cost	$110 per person per day

Unit 3 What do you say? 1 Page 15

Axa

Name: Axa
Kind of company: services
Industry: insurance
Nationality: French
Based in: France
Headquarters: Paris

Unit 12 What do you say? 2 Page 57

Student A

Hei Ping Tan

University/College: University of Beijing, China (1982–86)

Qualifications: Degree in computer science (1986)

First job: Computer teacher at the University of Beijing (1986–92)

Second job: Computer technician with China Unicom, a mobile phone company (1992–97)

Second qualification: Masters degree in business information systems, University of New South Wales, Australia (1998–9)

Current job: Computer support officer; help to set up computer programmes for research at University of Shanghai, China (1999–now)

Unit 12 Task 3 Page 59

Student A

As candidate, give the following information about yourself and your job experience.

2000: Degree in geography

2000–2002: Two years travelling around Europe, working in hotels and restaurants.

2002: Joined CultureTravel, a small company specialising in tours to historic cities, art and architecture tours.

2002–5: Worked for CultureTravel in the sales team.

2005–now: Leader of the sales team, you are responsible for 6 people.

Skills: IT skills, website design; languages (English, French)

You want a new job because you would like to work for a bigger company and develop your career in the travel industry.

Unit 14 Task 1 Page 66

	Monday	Tuesday	Wednesday	Thursday	Friday
am	Prepare for a visit from Canadian clients	10.00 Give clients a tour of our factory	Take clients on a sightseeing tour of the city	8.30 Hold meeting with the team to discuss the visit	Take the day off
pm	Clients arrive 6pm. Meet them at airport	Evening Have dinner with clients at restaurant	5.15 Clients depart		

Unit 15 Task 3 Page 73

Group A

Subject of presentation: Project costs for the next three months

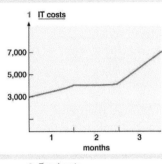

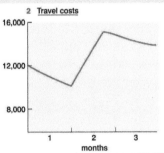

Unit 12 Task 3 Page 59

Student B

As candidate, give the following information about yourself and your job experience.

2003: Left school (you didn't go to university)

2003-4: Worked for a mobile phone store as a sales assistant. (You attended a company sales training programme)

2004: Left the job because you wanted to travel. One year travelling to India, Australia and the US.

2005: Joined Global Travel. Worked as sales assistant in a branch office.

2006: You were Sales Person of the Year in this company.

2007: Promoted to Branch Manager, responsible for 10 people. You still work in this job.

Skills: Good people skills, good IT skills. You are learning English.

You want a new job because you would like to do something different. You would like to travel in your work.

Unit 1 Task 3 Page 9

Student B

Visitor information

Name: Angela Jenkins

Company: Oil Quest Inc

To see: Mrs Horrocks (factory manager)

Unit 2 Task 2 Page 12

Group B

Web designer

Responsibility: company website

Activities: manage and maintain the website; design pages for the website

Unit 3 Task 2 Page 16

Student B

Company: Zagwing (manufactures small aeroplanes)

Subsidiaries: 15

Factories: 2

Employees: 950

Sales: 220 million euros

Unit 3 What do you say? 1 Page 15

Hyundai

Name: Hyundai

Kind of company: manufacturing

Industry: cars

Nationality: South Korean

Based in: South Korea

Headquarters: Seoul

Unit 9 Task 1 Page 43

Student B

Child's sports tricycle

Height = 55 cm   Length = 146 cm

Width = 68 cm   Weight = 16 kg

Unit 2   Task 2   Page 12

Group B

IT project manager

Responsibility: IT projects

Activities: plan projects; control the budget; co-ordinate the project team

Unit 3   Task 3   Page 17

Student B

Company: Seto – an insurance company
Sells: insurance services
Headquarters: Tokyo, Japan
Subsidiaries: 19
Number of offices: 199 (159 in Japan, 40 in other countries)
Employees: 7,000
Sales: 4 billion yen
CEO: Miko Ishiguro

Unit 4   Task 2   Page 22

Student B

1 You need a letter from Mr Walenska. Location: in-tray – under other letters.
2 You need a file with the name 'Budget'. Location: filing cabinet – top drawer.
3 You need the computer manual. Location: bookcase – bottom shelf.

Unit 6   Task 1   Page 29

Student B

Supplier
(100 cents = one dollar / $1)
Apples – $0.80 / kilo
Beef – $16 / kilo
Mineral water – $0.45 / litre
Tomatoes – $0.35 / tin (500 grams)
Potatoes – $0.30 / kilo
Milk – $0.50 / litre

Unit 6   Task 2   Page 30

Student B

Supplier
This is what you have/don't have in stock:
- G500 Photo Printer – you have 5 in stock. Price: $150
- Printer cartridges – you have 8 multi-colour cartridges in stock.
- Photo paper – you have 4 packs in stock.
- Bluetooth adapter – out of stock
- Folders (for photos) – you have 20 in stock.

Unit 6   Task 3   Page 31

Student B

Supplier Price list
Envelopes
EVWA4 (White A4, pack of 500): $9.20
EVWA5 (White A5, pack of 500): $8.45
EVBA4 (Brown A4, pack of 500): $6.60

Paper for photocopier
CP804 (White A4, pack of 500 sheets): $11.25
CP803 (White A3, pack of 500 sheets): $19. 99

Printer cartridges
GE490 (Black): $8.49 each
JA685 (Multi-colour): $44.60 each

Desk diaries
DDQ07 (Executive desk diary): $15.25 each
DDK07 (Standard desk diary): $11.80 each

Unit 6   Task 3   Page 31

Student B

Buyer
Customer details
Name: Sam Quirk
Company name: YTS Motors
Customer account number: 825437

Unit 2   Task 2   Page 12

Group B

IT service engineer

Responsibility: all computer systems in the company

Activities: build and set up computers; repair computers and computer equipment

Unit 7   Task 3   Page 37

Student B

Today is 1st January

Project: To produce a new sales catalogue

Agree the budget: beginning of August

Discuss ideas for the design: end of August

Write product descriptions: September

Take photos: 10th October

The design department prepares the pages: October–November

Send the catalogue to the printers: 30th November

Printers deliver the catalogues: 16th December

Send copies to customers: 27th December

Unit 11   Task 3   Page 55

Student B

Centre B: Budapest

Accommodation	Rooms for 1,500 people
Exhibition space	3,000 square metres
From the airport	15 km (30 minutes by taxi or bus)
Special feature	Excellent food
Cost	$160 per person per day

Unit 14   Task 2   Page 68

Student A

You have a problem with your laptop. You would like Terry to look at it. You need it tomorrow for a presentation. Give your own name and phone number or invent them.

Unit 9   Task 2   Page 45

Student B

Product 2 Coffee warmer
Keeps your coffee warm (60 degrees centigrade) when you are working at your PC
Made of metal
Size: Height = 20mm, width = 100mm
Why special: you plug it into your PC
Price: €21.45

Product 4 Portable chair
Take it camping or to the beach
Made of wood
Size (in the bag): height = 40cm, width = 10 cm, weight = 985gm
Why special: light and easy to carry, you can be comfortable anywhere
Price: €49.95

Unit 10   Task 2   Page 50

Student B

Part 1

- Greet your partner. Ask how he /she is.
- Answer your partner's question: You aren't enjoying the new job; finding the work difficult, missing your old colleagues.
- Ask about Frank.
- Ask about Darlene and Federico.
- Send greetings to them.

Part 2

- Greet your partner. Ask how he/she is.
- Ask: How is your new job?
- Answer question about Stella: hoping to work in marketing; applying for jobs.
- Answer question about Carlos and Ugo: working hard; travelling a lot.

Unit 1   Task 2   Page 8

Student B

Name	Quentin Yerxa
Company	Klinger and Rayburn
Job	Lawyer
Nationality	American

Student B

Hotel Waterside

A large modern hotel with four stars

600 rooms

Near the airport – the location isn't interesting

Far from the city centre

The hotel has two restaurants, a swimming pool and a gym

Your room: large, quiet

Price for the room: €190 (too expensive)

Student B

Claude Naudet

University / College: University of Toulouse, France (1991–1995)

Qualification: Degree in economics (1995)

First job: In the finance team at Computacenter (based in Toulouse) (1996–1999)

Second job: IBM France, in the finance department in Paris (2000–2005)

Second qualification Diploma in financial management, Lyon Business School (2005–2006)

Current job: Finance manager with IBM France. Responsible for 40 people (2006–now)

Student C

Centre C: Tokyo	
Accommodation	Rooms for 5,000 people
Exhibition space	20,000 square metres
From the airport	20 km (15 minutes by train)
Special feature	Very modern with the latest technology
Cost	$380 per person per day

	Monday	Tuesday	Wednesday	Thursday	Friday	Saturday
am	Fly to Mexico City Leave at 7.15 am	8.00 Meet with Señor García	8.30 IT team present new plans Have lunch with Pilar Ruiz	Attend a conference in Cancún	→	
pm	Arrive at 7.00 pm	2.00 Visit transport agents	4.30 Fly to Cancún			7.30 Fly home

Unit 2 Task 2 Page 12

Group A

Advertising manager

Responsibility: advertising company products

Activities: work with advertising companies; have meetings with the marketing team; manage projects

Unit 8 Task 3 Page 41

Student B

Correct procedure for problem 1

1 Plug in the laptop and projector.
2 Don't turn them on!
3 Connect the laptop to the projector [see picture].
4 Turn on the projector first and wait 60 seconds.
5 Then turn on the laptop.
6 Press the input button on the projector.

(**Solution:** A turned the laptop on first and then connected it to the projector.)

Unit 14 Task 2 Page 68

Student B

You have an interview with Monika Diski on Thursday at 3.45 pm. You would like to come another day if possible. Give your own name and phone number or invent them.

Unit 15 Task 3 Page 73

Group B

Subject of presentation: Marketing costs for the next three months

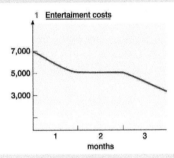

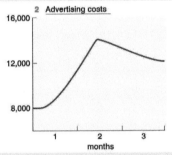

Unit 14 Task 3 Page 69

	Monday	Tuesday	Wednesday	Thursday	Friday
am		Conference		9.00-11.30 Meeting with project team	
pm	Travel north for a conference	Return in evening			Start holidays (leave after lunch)

Audioscripts

Kevin: Hello. I'm Kevin Morris. I'm from the UK.

Liisa: I'm Liisa Davidsson, from Finland. Nice to meet you. Gavin Morris?

Kevin: It's not Gavin, it's Kevin.

Liisa: Sorry, it's a difficult name for me! Can you spell it?

Kevin: K-E-V-I-N.

Liisa: Ah – Kevin!

Hans: Good morning.

Kevin + Liisa: Good morning.

Hans: Can I introduce myself? My name is Hans Bauer. I'm a sales manager from Germany.

Kevin: Hello! I'm Kevin Morris and I'm also a sales manager, from the UK.

Hans: Nice to meet you, Mr Morris.

Kevin: And this is Ms, er, sorry, can you say your name again?

Liisa: Liisa Davidsson, from Finland. Nice to meet you.

Hans: Nice to meet you, too. Are you a sales manager, too, Ms Davidsson?

Liisa: No, I'm not. I'm a finance manager.

Unit 1 **Listening 2** page 8 (CD track 2)

Alex Markov: Good morning. My name's Alexander Markov. I'm here to see Mrs Brown.

Receptionist: Good morning, Mr ... Sorry. Can you say your name again?

Alex Markov: Markov. M-A-R-K-O-V.

Receptionist: And your company name?

Alex Markov: I'm not with a company. I'm a student.

Receptionist: Oh, right. Now, you want to see Mrs Brown. Is that Sonia Brown or Julia Brown?

Alex Markov: Oh, I'm not sure.

Receptionist: What's her job?

Alex Markov: She's a personnel manager. I'm here about a job.

Receptionist: OK. That's Julia Brown. Just a moment. I'll call her. ...
Hello? It's Reception here. Mr Alexander Markov is here to see Julia Brown. ...
Oh, she isn't? OK. ...
I'm sorry. She isn't in her office at the moment. She's in a meeting. Can you wait about ten minutes?

Alex Markov: Yes, of course.

Receptionist: Please have a seat.

Alex Markov: Thank you.

Receptionist: Oh, and here's your visitor's badge.

Alex Markov: Thank you.

Unit 2 **Listening 1** page 10 (CD track 3)

Introduction 1

A: Hi, everyone! This is my friend Suzanne. She's from Australia. She lives in Sydney but she's on a world tour right now. She likes travelling and visiting different countries.

Introduction 2

B: Good morning. Can I introduce Akiro Watanabe. Mr Watanabe is from Japan and he works for Toshiba in the marketing department. He's interested in our packaging designs.

Unit 2 **Listening 2** page 12 (CD track 4)

Milos: Good morning. I'm Milos Hesko from Slovakia.

Janine: Good morning. Nice to meet you. I'm Janine Parks. I'm the sales manager and I'm in charge of the sales department. Can I introduce the sales team? This is Fiona Quigley.

Milos: Good morning.

Fiona: Pleased to meet you.

Janine: And this is Ben Thomas.

Milos: Nice to meet you.

Ben: Good morning.

Milos: Fiona and Ben are both sales representatives. Fiona is responsible for sales in the north and Ben is responsible for sales in the south. They travel a lot and visit customers. And this is Wayne Carr.

Milos: Good morning.

Wayne: Hello.

Janine: Wayne is responsible for customer services. He works in the office. He deals with problems and answers questions from customers. This is Zoe James, the department secretary. She is responsible for communication in the team. She answers the telephone, takes messages and arranges team meetings.

Milos: Hello.

Zoe: Hello.

Janine: And Gina Scott is a conference organiser. She organises our sales conferences.

Milos: Hello.

Gina: Nice to meet you.

Janine: Right, now you all know each other, let's ...

Unit 3 **Listening 1** page 15 (CD track 5)

A: My company is called Posies. It's a retail company and it sells clothing.

B: I work for Hassel. It's an insurance company and it's based in Switzerland.

C: I'm with Rexoil – it's a petroleum company. I work in the UK subsidiary, but the headquarters are in the US.

D: And I work for Kim Sung. We manufacture computers. We are based in South Korea but we have subsidiaries in many countries.

Unit 3 **Listening 2** page 15 (CD track 6)

Pascual: My company is called Delicias. It's a food production company. It's based in Chile, in South America, but we have thirteen subsidiaries in different countries in north and south America.

Helen: Sorry, is that thirteen or thirty?

Pascual: Thirteen. One-three.

Helen: Thirteen. Right.

Pascual: Then factories ... we have five factories in Chile and seven in other countries.

Helen: So, that's twelve factories?

Pascual: Sorry, no. It's not twelve, it's eleven. There are four factories in Chile, not five. So that's eleven factories.

Helen: And how many employees do you have?

Pascual: About seven thousand.

Helen: Sorry, can you say that again?

Pascual: Seven thousand.

Helen: OK. And what about your sales?

Pascual: Er, in US dollars, our sales are about eight hundred million.

Helen: Can you repeat that number, please?

Pascual: Eight hundred million US dollars.

Unit 4 **Listening 1** page 21 (CD track 7)

Eva: Hello?

Michaela: Hello, Eva? It's Michaela. I'm in a meeting with the finance manager and I need a very important document – a report on office communications.

Eva: OK.

Michaela: Can you please find it and bring it to me in the meeting room? I'm sorry but I can't leave the meeting at the moment.

Eva: No problem. Where is the report?

Michaela: Go into my office. Behind my desk there's a filing cabinet.

Eva: Right.

Michaela: The filing cabinet has three drawers. Open the top drawer of the filing cabinet.

Eva: Yes.

Michaela: Look in a file with the name 'New Projects'.

Eva: 'New Projects'.

Michaela: The report is in that file. Please don't bring the file. Just bring the report.

Eva: OK. I'll do it now.

Michaela: Thank you, Eva!

Unit 4 **What do you say? 2** Page 22 (CD track 8)

Part 1

This is a repeat of the first part of Eva's conversation with Michaela (to '... Where is the report?') from *Listening 1*.

Unit 4 **What do you say? 2** Page 22 (CD track 9)

Part 2

This is a repeat of the second part of Eva's conversation with Michaela (from '... go into my office?') from *Listening 1*.

Alain: Hello?

Kathy: Hi, Alain, it's Kathy. Are you still joining us tonight?

Alain: Hello. Yes, of course.

Kathy: Great. Well, we're meeting for dinner at the Hong Kong restaurant. Do you know it?

Alain: No, I don't. Could you tell me where it is?

Kathy: Well, it's in the town centre near the train station.

Alain: That's good because I will arrive by train.

Kathy: OK, so come out of the train station. Turn right and go along Station Road. Go past the Station Hotel.

Alain: Right along Station Road, OK.

Kathy: Yes. Take the first turning left after the Station Hotel and you're in River Street. The river is on your right.

Alain: OK. River Street.

Kathy: Go straight on. The restaurant is on the corner of George Street.

Alain: Fine. Thank you for your help.

Kathy: No problem. See you tonight.

Waiter: Are you ready to order?

Georgio: Yes, we are.

Waiter: What would you like to start with?

Georgio: We'd like two soups, please.

Waiter: Two soups. OK. And for the main course?

Rossana: Can I have the salmon, please?

Waiter: Salmon. Certainly. Would you like potatoes with that?

Rossana: No potatoes, thank you. Just a salad, please. But no tomatoes – I'm sorry, but I don't like tomatoes.

Waiter: Salad with no tomatoes. OK. And for you, sir?

Georgio: I'd like roast lamb, please.

Waiter: Roast lamb. Would you like any vegetables or side dishes?

Georgio: What vegetables do you have?

Waiter: We have peas, carrots, roast potatoes and fried potatoes.

Georgio: Roast potatoes, please.

Waiter: OK, so that's two soups, one salmon with salad and one roast lamb with roast potatoes. Anything else?

Georgio: Can you bring some water, please?

Waiter: Certainly.

Magda: It's a lovely restaurant. Do you often come here?

Stephen: Not often, because it's a long way from the office. But I like it here – the food is always excellent.

Magda: Yes, the menu looks very good.

Stephen: What would you like?

Magda: I don't know – it's difficult to choose. What do you recommend?

Stephen: I can recommend the trout. It's a local speciality.

Magda: Sorry, but I don't know 'trout' – what is it?

Stephen: It's a kind of fish – from the river.

Magda: That's good. I like fish very much. I'd like to try it.

Stephen: And would you like vegetables with that?

Magda: Yes, please.

Stephen: What about potatoes? Would you like roast or fried potatoes? And how about some ...?

Stephen: ... so we often have visitors from Poland. Ah! Here's the food!

Stephen: Thank you.

Magda: Thank you.

Stephen: Well, enjoy your meal!

Magda: Thank you ...

Stephen: Do you like your trout?

Magda: It's delicious, thank you. Everything is very good!

Stephen: Good, I'm glad. How about some more water?

Magda: Oh, no, thank you.

Conversation 1

Salesperson 1: Good morning, Stationery Plus. Alberto speaking. How can I help?

Silvio: Hello. This is Silvio Santana. I'd like to buy some printer cartridges, please. I need U3Z colour cartridges.

Salesperson 1: Certainly. How many would you like?

Silvio: I'd like twenty, please.

Salesperson 1: Just a moment ... I'm sorry. We only have ten in stock at the moment.

Silvio: Oh. How much are they?

Salesperson 1: Fifty euros each.

Silvio: OK – I'll think about it. Thank you.

Conversation 2

Salesperson 2: Good morning. Quest Suppliers. Can I help you?

Silvio: Good morning. This is Silvio Santana. I'd like to buy some printer cartridges, please. I need U3Z colour cartridges. Do you have any in stock at the moment?

Salesperson 2: I'm sorry, we don't have any at the moment – we're out of stock.

Silvio: Oh, OK. Thanks.

Conversation 3

Salesperson 3: Good morning. Plentiful Supplies. How can I help?

Silvio: Good morning. This is Silvio Santana. I'd like to buy some printer cartridges, please. I need U3Z colour cartridges. Do you have any in stock at the moment?

Salesperson 3 Yes, we have.

Silvio: How much are they?

Salesperson 3 Forty euros each. How many would you like?

Silvio: I'd like twenty, please.

Salesperson 3 OK, no problem. Would you like them today?

Silvio: Yes, please.

Unit 7   Listening page 35 (CD track 14)

Jack Delaney: I'd like to tell you about a project to buy some new paintings for the bank's head office.

First, I discussed the idea with the board of directors. Everyone thought it was a good idea. So then we looked at the finances and we agreed a budget of three million dollars for the project.

Next I set up a project team. I asked three people to be responsible for choosing the paintings. Their task was to complete the project within three months and to stay within the budget.

Then, in the next two months, the project team visited different art galleries and looked at all the options. They had regular meetings to discuss their ideas and to choose the paintings they wanted to buy.

After that they presented their choices to the board. The board agreed, and finally, we ordered the paintings.

Unit 8   Listening 1 page 38 (CD track 15)

Receptionist: Hello, Reception.

Rita: Hello. This is Rita da Silva from room 101. I have a problem with the television.

Receptionist: Oh, dear, what's the problem?

Rita: I think there's something wrong with it. I can't turn it on.

Receptionist: Oh. Did you plug it in?

Rita: Yes, I did.

Receptionist: And did you press the button to turn it on?

Rita: Yes, I pressed the button but nothing happened. It doesn't work. I think it's broken.

Receptionist: I'm very sorry about that. I'll ask someone to come and have a look at it.

Rita: Thank you.

Unit 8   What do you say? 1 page 39 (CD track 15)

This is a repeat of the conversation from *Listening 1*.

Unit 8   Listening 2 page 40 (CD track 16)

Steve: Computer workshop, Steve speaking. How can I help?

Fred: Hello, Steve. It's Fred here. I have this new computer and I think there's something wrong with it. I can't check my email.

Steve: OK, don't worry. I'm sure we can fix it. What did you do?

Fred: The usual things. First, I turned it on. Then I connected to the internet, and then I clicked on the email icon. I tried to check my mail – but nothing happened.

Steve: When you clicked on email, what did you see on the screen?

Fred: Er, there was a box and it asked me for my user name and password.

Steve: And did you type your password?

Fred: Yes, I did.

Steve: Did you type your user name, too?

Fred: Yes, I did.

Steve: What did you type?

Fred: Fred Smith – that's my name.

Steve: So, you didn't type your user name.

Fred: What's my user name?

Steve: It's usually your email address.

Fred: Oh, I didn't know that. I didn't type my email address.

Steve: Well, that's why you couldn't check your email. You didn't type your email address. Try it again now.

Fred: OK … wait a moment … . Oh! That's it! You fixed it! Thank you for your help, Steve!

Steve: No problem, Fred.

Unit 9   Listening page 44 (CD track 17)

Brian: Hello. I'm Brian Thorpe and I'd like to tell you about a great new product, the Magic Egg Cooker. As you can tell from the name, you use it for cooking eggs. It cooks eggs perfectly every time without any water. Let me show you how it works. You put the eggs in here – you can cook up to six eggs at the same time, but they must be the same size. You plug the egg cooker in, turn it on … like this … and wait for the eggs to cook. The egg cooker sets the time automatically. It is made of strong plastic and it's easy to clean. It's small and light, just 20 centimetres long and 12 centimetres wide. So you can easily find space for it in your kitchen … OK – that means the eggs are ready. Let's have a look … there you are! A perfect egg!

Unit 10   Listening 1 page 49 (CD track 18)

Gerald: Hello, Regina! Good to see you.

Regina: Hi, Gerald. How are you? You're looking well.

Gerald: I'm very well, thanks. And you?

Regina: Oh, I'm fine. How's business?

Gerald: It's great. We're getting lots of orders for our new model – the 498.

Regina: That's good! Are you ready for the launch in Japan?

Gerald: Yes, nearly. Our salespeople are preparing the publicity. They're working on a new DVD in Japanese.

Regina: Sounds interesting.

Gerald: And how's Miranda? Is she still working with you?

Regina: Yes, she is. She's fine. She's working hard but she's enjoying the work – and learning a lot.

Gerald: Oh, good. Well, give her my regards.

Regina: I will.

Gerald: Let's go to my office. There's something I want to show you …

Unit 10   Listening 2 page 51 (CD track 19)

Part 1

William: OK – so this is our warehouse. This is where we store the coffee beans. Look – a truck is just arriving. It's delivering new supplies of coffee beans.

Una: Where do the beans come from?

William: They're mostly from the Caribbean, from Jamaica.

Una: Oh, really?

Part 2

William: And this is where we process the beans. That machine there is roasting beans right now.

Una: Hmm – I can smell them. It's a lovely smell! And what's that man doing?

William: That's Joe. He's checking the colour of the roasted beans. When the colour is right, we know the beans are ready.

Una: And what's happening over there?

William: We usually use that machine for grinding the roasted beans. But it isn't working at the moment. Alicia – what's the problem here?

Alicia: The machine isn't grinding the beans very well – the grounds are too big. I'm trying to repair it.

Part 3

William: And now the final part of the process – quality control. This is where we taste the coffee. This is Martina.

Una: Hello, Martina!

Martina: Hello.

William: Martina is preparing cups of coffee to taste. And Bruno here …

Una: Hello, Bruno!

Bruno: Hi!

William: Bruno is tasting the coffee, to see if the quality is good. Would you like to try some, Una?

Una: Yes, please. Thank you. Hmm – it's delicious!

Unit 11 Listening page 55 (CD track 20)

Part 1

Nico: OK, the next point is to choose a conference centre for our next conference. So, first, let's think about what we need. What about size? Jacques, how much accommodation do we need?

Jacques: We need accommodation for one thousand five hundred people. So, we need a big conference centre, but not too big.

Nico: One thousand five hundred. OK.

Pauline: And last year, we didn't have enough exhibition space. That was a problem.

Nico: How much space do we need, Pauline?

Pauline: Three thousand square metres. That's the minimum!

Nico: Three thousand square metres.

Unit 11 Listening page 55 (CD track 21)

Part 2

Nico: OK. What else do we need? What facilities are important?

Pauline: In my opinion, the most important thing is to have a modern conference centre with good equipment and the latest technology.

Jacques: Yes, I agree.

Nico: OK. Jacques – any other ideas?

Jacques: It's important that people can get there easily. So we want the conference centre to be near the airport.

Nico: Near the airport. OK. Anything else?

Jacques: Good restaurants!

Pauline: Yes, I agree. Last year, the food was awful! We must do better this year!

Unit 12 Listening 1 page 57 (CD track 22)

Matt: Well, I studied business administration at university from 1995 to 1999 and I have a masters degree in business. My first job was with Smartex, a retail company based in the UK. I worked there as an assistant store manager. Then, in 2001, I left Smartex and joined Market World, a big international retail company. After two years there, the company offered me a job as a store manager in a new store in Indonesia and I accepted.

I stayed there for two years. It was an excellent experience and I learned a lot! But my girlfriend was in England and I wanted to come back and get married. So, I came back in November 2005, and I worked as the general manager in a Liverpool store – still with Market World. We got married in June 2006. And in October 2007, the company promoted me to be the regional manager for the north west. And I'm still in that job now. I've worked in retailing for a long time and I really enjoy it.

Unit 12 Listening 2 page 58 (CD track 23)

Ken: Hi. Please come in. You're Inga Muller, is that right?

Inga: That's right.

Ken: Thanks for coming, Inga. Please take a seat.

Inga: Thank you.

Ken: So – can you tell me a bit about yourself?

Inga: Well, I studied geography at university. And I like travelling very much – that's why I decided to work in the airline industry.

Ken: How long have you worked in the airline industry?

Inga: For five years. I started at EuropAir – I worked in their operations team at Hamburg airport for a year. And then I joined Hi-Fly, the new economy airline.

Ken: And have you been responsible for a team of people before?

Inga: Yes – at Hi Fly, I joined the management training programme. And since then I've worked as an operations manager. At the moment, I'm responsible for a team of eight people.

Ken: So, why do you want this job?

Inga: Because Hi-Fly is a small company and I would like to work for a big airline at a big airport. I really want to develop my skills as a manager. And also it's a great opportunity to work in a different country and to use my English.

Ken: Have you ever lived in a foreign country?

Inga: Yes, I have. I spent one year in Philadelphia.

Ken: Oh, right. So you've lived in the US before. When was that?

Inga: Just after I left school. I stayed with an American family and went to a college to improve my English.

Ken: And what special skills do you have?

Inga: I speak three languages: German, English and French. And I have good IT skills.

Ken: And what do you want to do in the future?

Inga: I plan to stay in the airline industry and to develop my career as a manager. At the same time, I'd like to ...

Unit 13 Listening page 64 (CD track 24)

Choi: OK. Welcome to the meeting, everyone. As you know, we are here to discuss how to improve the health and fitness of the employees. One problem is that five out of twenty employees smoke cigarettes. It isn't good for their health. Should we do something to help them stop? What do people think? Sam, what do you think?

Sam: Well, at the moment, it's too easy to go to the smoking room and have a cigarette. Why don't we close the smoking room – so there's no smoking inside the building?

Choi: OK. That's a good idea. Any other ideas? Pippa?

Pippa: I've heard that there are courses to help people stop smoking. Why don't we send the smokers on one of those courses?

Justine: I don't think that's a good idea. We can't make people go on a course.

Choi: You're right, Justine.

Pippa: OK, we can't make people go. But perhaps we could advise people to go. We could tell people about the courses, and they could go during working hours if they want to.

Sam: And perhaps we could pay for the course, too.

Pippa: Yes, I like that idea!

Justine: I'm not sure about that. I think we should find out how much the courses cost, because they could be very expensive.

Choi: I agree. Justine, would you like to get some information about the stop-smoking courses and find out about the cost?

Justine: OK.

Choi: Thank you, Justine. OK, let's go on to the next problem.

Unit 14 Listening 1 page 67 (CD track 25)

Receptionist: Connex. Good morning.

Jane: Oh, good morning. This is Jane Kelly from Greenshanks. Can I speak to David Potts, please?

Receptionist: I'm afraid he isn't in the office this morning. Would you like to speak to his assistant?

Jane: Yes, please.

Receptionist: Just a moment, please.

Paul: Hello. Paul Ardetti.

Jane: Hello. This is Jane Kelly from Greenshanks.

Paul: Oh, yes.

Jane: I'm trying to contact David Potts, but I understand he isn't in the office this morning.

Paul: That's right. Can I take a message?

Jane: Well, I'm calling about your new brochure. I've got some samples to show Mr Potts. And I'd like to arrange a meeting with him.

Paul: It's probably best if you talk to him directly. Can he call you back this afternoon?

Jane: Well – OK. But I'm leaving the office at 3 o'clock.

Paul: That's not a problem. I can ask him to call you before 3. Can you give me your number?

Jane: It's 084 671 920.

Paul: 084 671 920.

Jane: Yes, that's right.

Paul: OK. I'll ask Mr Potts to call you this afternoon.

Jane: Thanks very much. Bye.

Paul: Bye.

Unit 14 Listening 2 page 69 (CD track 26)

Jane: Jane Kelly. Good afternoon.

David: Good afternoon. This is David Potts from Connex. I had a message to call you.

Jane: Oh, hello! Thanks for calling me back. I have some samples for the new brochure to show you.

David: Yes, that's great.

Jane: Can we meet? I can come to your office if you like.

David: OK. What's a good day for you?

Jane: How about tomorrow?

David: I'm afraid I'm busy tomorrow. Just a moment. Let me look at my schedule. Er, are you free next Monday?

Jane: Oh, I'm sorry. I'm working with the photographers on Monday.

David: Well, what about Tuesday?

Jane: Tuesday's fine. What time?

David: Nine o'clock?

Jane: I'm afraid I can't make nine o'clock. But I could come at nine thirty.

David: OK then. I'll see you at nine thirty on Tuesday.

Jane: That's good. See you then. Bye!

David: Goodbye.

Unit 15   Listening 1 page 71 (CD track 27)

Part 1

Lee: Good morning, everyone. I'd like to talk about the future of HQV and the opportunities for our company. First, I'll talk about the market for this technology in the next five years. Then I'll give you a forecast of sales for our HQV models. And finally, I'll present the price trend for this product.

Unit 15   Listening 1 page 71 (CD track 28)

Part 2

Lee: So, first, the market. As you know, this is a new technology and a new market. And as with any new technology, the market will increase slowly at first but then it will develop quickly. We are certain that the market for this technology will continue to go up for the next five years at least. After that, we could see other new technologies take over, but ...

Now let's look at the sales forecast for our new model. As you can see from the graph, sales will rise quickly in the second year but are likely to reach a peak in the third year. Why will sales reach a peak so soon when we know that the market will continue to increase for the next five years? The reason is that in the first year, we are the only company to offer this technology. So we will have one hundred per cent of the market share. But – other companies are certain to enter the market, and competition from these companies will increase. It is unlikely that we will be able to keep a one hundred per cent market share for long ...

Now I'd like to present the price trend for this technology. This graph shows that we will enter the market at a high price: three thousand five hundred dollars. We can set the price because we are the only company that is offering this technology. So, the price will remain steady at first, but will go down after a year or two as other competitors enter the market. We think that prices on the market will probably fall to about nine hundred dollars after five years. But by then we will probably be ready to launch the next generation of TVs!

So, that is our forecast for the market, the sales and the price trend. Do you have any questions?

Unit 15   Listening 2 page 73 (CD track 29)

This is a repeat of Lee's presentation in *Listening 1*.

Writing 5   Task 1 page 75 (CD track 30)

Assistant: Hello. Ron Brady's office.

Tara: Hello. This is Tara Leone from the north east regional sales office. Can I speak to Ron Brady if he's there, please?

Assistant: I'm sorry. He's in a meeting at the moment.

Tara: OK, can you give him a message, please?

Assistant: Yes, of course.

Tara: I'm calling back about the regional sales meeting. Can you tell him that the best date for me is the 18th March? The 14th March is also a possibility for me, but only after 9.30am.

Assistant: OK. So the 18th March is the best date, but you can come on the 14th March after 9.30am?

Tara: Yes, that's right. Oh, and can you tell him that I'll send my sales forecasts by email tomorrow?

Assistant: OK. I'll tell him.

Tara: Thanks. Bye.

Assistant: Bye.